50 AWARDED ARCHITECTURE

DESIGN MEDIA PUBLISHING LIMITED

Contents

Liljeholmen Shopping Mall

Designer: Equator Stockholm AB **Location:** Stockholm, Sweden **Completion date:** 2010 **Photographer:** Max Plunger

This mixed-use project, where public services, retail, offices and housing are integrated to create a new city node for local residents is a key in integrating the area into Stockholm's city centre. It is the first shopping centre in Europe to reach LEED platinum for its strong environmental profile.

In order to develop the area and achieve an urban feeling it has been important to add and integrate housing and to expand commerce and places of work. The successful development is based on this complex integrated functional puzzle solved through innovative solutions and turning challenges into successful key assets. In spite of challenging topographic conditions the huge potential of the location could be unlocked, and a "sprawl" area is now replaced by a lively city quarter, creating social sustainability. The project has been developed without any public funding and used the new "three-dimensional" zoning law, making it possible to optimise the built area of the new development. Liljeholmstorget has a unique location connected to an existing public transportation node with subway, tram and bus systems meet. The new additions to the area are defined around a new shopping mall, integrated with an existing office building containing public services.

On top of the shopping mall, the new apartments are placed around a green courtyard. The loading dock located further up the adjacent street is covered by a "green" roof using different plants to create an artistic pattern for the neighbors who look at it from the top of the hill. A new parking garage located in rock caverns is buried in the hill below the existing residential towers thus maximising the land-use.

The project's integrated functions allow synergies very beneficial to sustainable development and great environmental ambitions have followed the entire process. Finding creative solutions for energy-saving and water consumption, efficient use of land, efficient waste and water management, avoiding non-environmentally friendly materials is how an LEED Platinum level has been achieved. Liljeholmstorget is a success story confirming that environmentally responsible strategy can go hand-in-hand with commercial success.

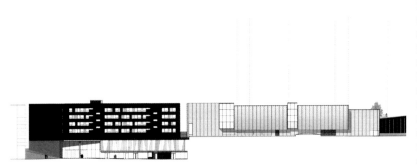

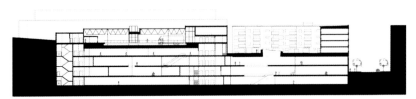

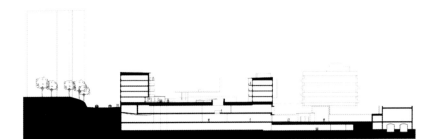

Top right: The square at night
Bottom right: The first LEED platinum shopping centre in Europe

Awarded:
Swedish Association of Architects Planning Award, 2010

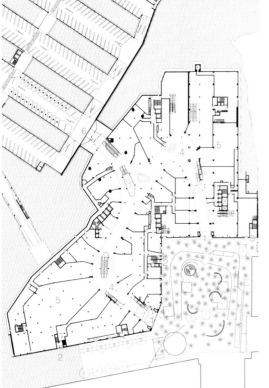

1. Mall entrance
2. Entrance to Housing
3. Entrance to community centre
4. Mall
5. Shop
6. Entrance from garage
7. Underground garage.

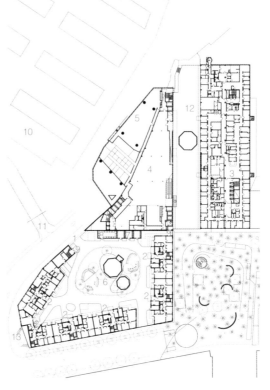

1. Access to courtyard
2. Entrance to Housing
3. Health care
4. Shop
5. Technical area
6. Green courtyard
7. Bicycle storage
8. Waste room
9. Emergency exit from mall
10. Underground garage
11. Garage exit
12. Green roof
13. Garage entrance

Top left: View from the highway
Top right: Housing courtyard
Bottom right: Aerial view of the loading dock

Portside

Designer: Arkhefield **Location:** Hamilton, Australia **Completion date:** 2006 **Photographer:** Scott Burrows / Aperture Photography

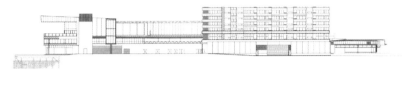

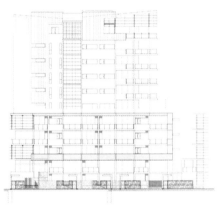

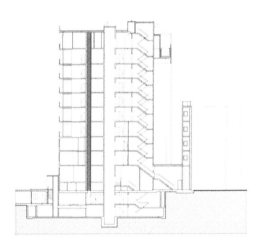

Right: Entrance

Portside is the redevelopment of a waterfront site adjacent to the Brisbane CBD. The site was previously a wharf for container shipping that had fallen dormant. In 2003, Arkhefield was awarded the project to redesign the site as the city's cruise ship terminal. The terminal is supported by accompanying commercial, retail and residential areas within a master planned development. The site is arranged around a central public plaza and street. This plaza links the surrounding suburb to the water as a diagonal slice through the site. The Cruise Terminal and accompanying retail, cinema and commercial spaces flank the eastern side of the plaza. The western side contains restaurants with a range of residential apartment buildings over. The project is staged with Stage 1 completed in 2006. At completion, the site will be an urban village housing over 1000 residents with all necessary amenities to support people's lifestyles. The existing wharves to the waterfront have been rejuvenated to create a 400-metre-long promenade. This promenade becomes the berthing platform on cruise ship days, farewelling and welcoming over 4000 passengers within a daily turnaround. The cruise terminal is a challenging design problem, in that the building needs to cater for large numbers of people on a weekly basis, and lie dormant for times in between cruise ship arrivals. The design embedded the functioning of the cruise terminal within the retail fabric to maintain a fully active ground plane year round. The public plaza is designed to cater for both the daily retail and residential occupations as well as very large crowds on cruise ship days. This was achieved by maximising the area of the ground plane, while also creating smaller intimate spaces for people to gather during normal weekdays.

Awarded:
2008 UDIA Queensland Awards – Retail Commercial
2008 UDIA Queensland Awards – Urban Renewal
Prestigious and highly sought-after in the Queensland development industry, the UDIA Queensland Awards for Excellence Programme is one of Queensland's most respected and valued industry awards programmes. The Awards have been developed specifically by and for the development industry to recognise excellence and innovation in one of the state's critical industry groups.
The Awards programme culminates in a spectacular gala dinner and presentation ceremony, which attracts a large and impressive audience of development professionals together with dignitaries including State Government ministers and members and mayors and councilors from across the Queensland.

PORTSIDE
WHARF
BRISBANE CRUISE TERMINAL
DENDY
CINEMAS
fresh n wild markets
bodywize
Function Centre
Restaurants
Retail

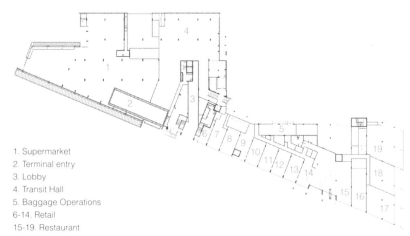

1. Supermarket
2. Terminal entry
3. Lobby
4. Transit Hall
5. Baggage Operations
6-14. Retail
15-19. Restaurant

Left: Commercial precinct
Right: Public plaza

Left: Cruise liner terminal

Barracks

Designer: Arkhefield **Location:** Paddington, Queensland, Australia **Completion date:** 2009
Photographer: Scott Burrows / Aperture Photography

The architecture of the development was conceived to enhance the already well-known landmark buildings and form a strong link with Caxton Street. The heritage buildings were re-furbished and new buildings were designed with respect to the site's heritage whilst providing distinctive new homes for prominent commercial, retail and cinema tenants. A strong pedestrian link was sought to connect Caxton Street to the city.

Positioning of pedestrian arrival points, cinema entry and supermarket entry activate the external malls and lanes at ground level which are inhabited by retail tenants. These external spaces between buildings were incorporated deliberately to create an inviting retail precinct of shops and open air dining and provide a continuation of the Caxton Street strip shops and restaurants.

The commercial component called for a new building which respects and connects to the heritage-listed Police Barracks building. This was achieved in a large, low building with a bridge to the old building on Petrie Terrace. An atrium was introduced to maximise natural light and enhance the quality of the large floor plate. Striking orange and red meeting "pods" were used to give the building prominence at the end of the city reach of the river.

The cinema was designed as a beacon for night-time entertainment. It has a faceted façade that follows the outline of the theatres inside as a counterpoint to the traditional forms of the heritage buildings. A large glass foyer takes advantage of city views and provides a visual link between diners in the mall and cinema patrons.

Careful consideration of the needs of Barracks patrons, major tenants, stadium access, car parking, and heritage constraints has resulted in a distinctive group of buildings which fit neatly within the scale of the Caxton Street area. The architecture works to present an attractive and inviting new retail and commercial precinct which will positively contribute to its neighbourhood.

1. Kitchen
2. Toilet
3. Restaurant
4. Tenancy 2
5. Tenancy 3
6. Tenancy 4
7. Tenancy 7

Awarded:
2010 UDIA National Awards — Urban Renewal
2009 UDIA Queensland Awards — Retail Commercial
2009 UDIA Queensland Awards — Urban Renewal

Right: Cinema

The Urban Development Institute of Australia's National Awards for Excellence celebrates Australia's contemporary knowledge, skills and innovation in the urban development industry. The awards recognise outstanding achievements of high-quality developments that contribute to the industry, government and community.

Left: Bar & Café

Bahrain World Trade Centre

Designer: Atkins **Location:** Manama, Bahrain **Completion date:** 2008 **Photographer:** Atkins

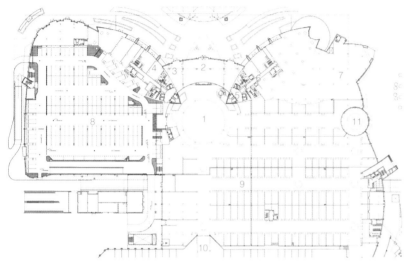

1. Centre court
2. Entrance lobby
3. Office lobby
4. Security
5. Lift lobby
6. Corridor
7. Anchor tenant
8. Parking
9. Mall
10. Existing mall
11. North court

Atkins was appointed to provide all masterplanning architecture and structural and MEP engineering design services for the Bahrain World Trade Centre site, located on the main King Faisal Highway in Manama, Bahrain. More than half of its area was previously developed, and comprised the Sheraton Bahrain Hotel, an associated single-storey luxury shopping mall, an office tower, car parking facilities, services and landscaped areas.

Designers from Atkins developed the master plan for the extended development that rejuvenates the existing mall and hotel and provides additional 50-storey twin office towers with unobstructed views over the Arabian Gulf, a new shopping mall with anchor tenant and several food outlets.

The focal point of the development is the twin triangular-shaped towers which sit above a sculpted three-storey podium. Tapering to a height of 240 metres, each tower is visually anchored to the ground by a concertina of curved, sail-like forms, and provides thirty-four floors of office space and an exclusive viewing deck on the 42nd floor.

Unique to this building and rising to the challenge of incorporating renewable energy solutions within sustainable architecture, the design includes three 29-metre-diametre wind turbines horizontally supported on bridges. The turbines are expected to produce between 11 and 15 percent of the total electrical consumption of the towers.

Research of many months, including extensive dialogue with turbine manufacturers, was conducted through the feasibility concept and design development stages of the project. Technical validation included computational fluid dynamics modelling, wind tunnel testing, vibration and acoustic assessments, electrical integration analysis and SARM analysis. Output from these was incorporated by design teams into an integrated building, bridge and turbine design. Atkins is also responsible for the supervision of construction.

The Bahrain World Trade Centre forms the focal point of a master plan to rejuvenate an existing hotel and shopping mall on a prestigious site overlooking the Arabian Gulf in the downtown central business district of Manama, Bahrain. The concept design of the Bahrain World Trade Centre towers was inspired by the traditional Arabian "Wind Towers" in that the very shape of the buildings harness the unobstructed prevailing onshore breeze from the Gulf, providing a renewable source of energy for the project.

The two 50-storey sail-shaped office towers taper to a height of 240 metres and support three 29-metre-diametre horizontal-axis wind turbines. The towers are harmoniously integrated on top of a three-storey sculpted podium and basement which accommodate a new shopping centre, restaurants, business centres and car parking.

The specific architectural forms of the Bahrain World Trade Centre towers were borne from using the nautical expression of a sail to harness the consistent onshore breeze, potentially to generate energy using wind dynamics, as well as to create two elegant towers for Bahrain, which would transcend time and become one of a kind in the world.

Right: The view of the main building seen from the entrance

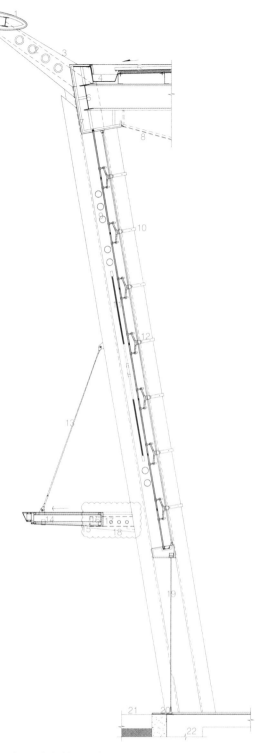

1. White composite metal cladding steel structure
2. Polished stainless steel pipes fixed to main steel structure
3. Steel brackets to structural drawings and details clad with white composite aluminium panels
4. 1.5mm thick GI sheet gutter all around
5. Proprietary profiled pre-insulated standing seam aluminium roofing panels
6. Steel structure specialist contractor
7. "Silver metallic" composite metal cladding panels
8. Ceiling to interior design details
9. Polished stainless steel CHS fixed to main steel structure
10. 10mm thick stainless steel plate fixed to the column main structure
11. Polished stainless steel bracing bars
12. Proprietary polished stainless steel point fixied on polished stainless brackets and tension structure
13. Polished stainless steel tension rods
14. Lights' drawings and details
15. Brushed "silver metallic" composite metal cladding to canopy to specification H31
16. Steel supporting frames to structural details
17. Polished stainless steel pipes
18. Steel supporting brackets to structural clad with white composite aluminium panels
19. Green tinted double glazed fixed glass panels
20. 30mm thick granite apron laid to fall
21. External finish to landscape
22. Centre line of columns on the ground floor

Left: Lighting effect at night
Right: Entrance

Awarded:

2006 LEAF Awards

2008 BEX Award / Innovation Category

2008 The Council on Tall Buildings and Urban Habitat Awards

2008 Construction Week Awards

The LEAF Awards is an international architectural prize, recognising innovative architectural design, across both private and public sectors. Entry is open to all architects worldwide and buildings can be anywhere in the world.

The LEAF Awards programme is operated by the Leading European Architects Forum (LEAF), founded in 2001. LEAF brings together leading international architectural practices and designers operating in Europe and beyond to share knowledge, to network and to develop new partnerships.

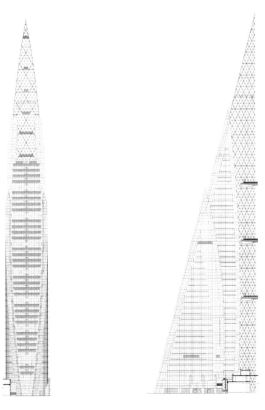

Shanghai World Financial Centre

Designer: KPF / William Pedersen **Location:** Shanghai, China **Completion date:** 2008
Photographer: KPF

The programme of this 95-storey project is contained within two distinctly formal elements: a sculpted tower and a podium. Corresponding to the Chinese concept of the earth as a square and the sky as a circle, the interaction between these two geometric forms gives shape to the tower. The project relates to its context through an abstract language that attempts symbolically to incorporate characteristics meaningful to the traditions of Chinese architecture, but is not limited to pictorial or image-based historical precedents. The primary form of the tower is a square prism intersected by two sweeping arcs, tapering into a single line at the apex. The gradual progression of floor plans generates configurations that are ideal for offices on the lower floors and hotel suites above. At the same time, the transformation of the plan rotates the orientation of the upper portion of the tower towards the Oriental Pearl TV Tower, the area's dominant landmark, a fifth of a mile away. To relieve wind pressure, a 50-metre opening is carved out of the top of the building. Equal in length to the sphere of the television tower, this void connects the two structures across the urban landscape. Wall, wing and conical forms penetrate through the massive stone base of the tower.

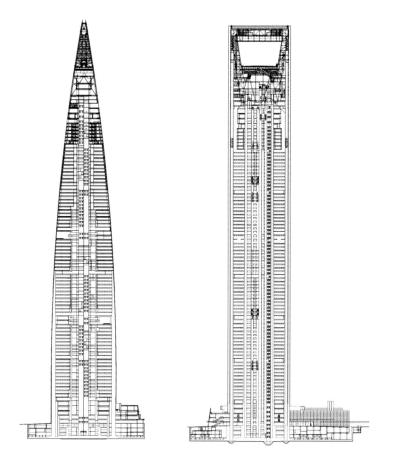

Awarded:
2008 Best Tall Building – Asia, Council on Tall Buildings and Urban Habitat
2008 Architectural Award – American Institute of Architects Hong Kong Chapter
2008 ACEC New York Diamond Award for Structural Systems
The American Council of Engineering Companies of New York (ACEC New York) is the voice of New York State's engineering companies. Whether for sole proprietors or global companies, for young principals or industry leaders, ACEC New York has, since its formation in 1921, been true to its mission: To be the leading advocate in New York State for consulting engineers and to enhance the image and business practices of professional engineering companies.
Boasting a membership of two hundred and seventy firms, including forty-three affiliate firms throughout the state, ACEC New York is a highly focused group that lobbies, advocates, educates, networks, provides scholarships for engineering students, and awards and recognises outstanding engineering efforts of its member firms.

Right: 101 storeys above the city skyline

Left: Recognised by the Council on Tall Buildings and Urban Habitat as the Best Tall Building in the World 2008
Right: A square prism — the symbol used by the ancient Chinese to represent the earth

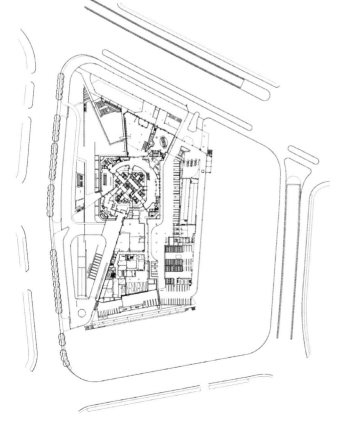

Designer: Foreign Office Architects **Location:** Leicester, UK **Completion date:** 2008 **Photographer:** Satoru Mishima, Peter Jeffree, Helene Binet & Lube Saveski

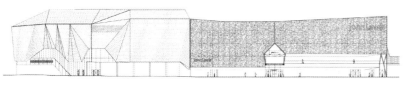

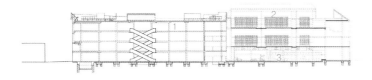

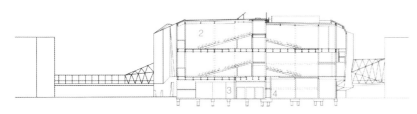

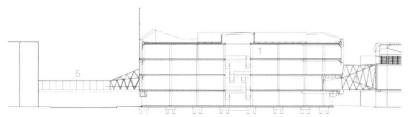

1. Department store
2. Cinema
3. Service yard
4. Retail
5. Public circulation

John Lewis Department Store and Cineplex

Commissioned within a larger city centre regeneration scheme, the Department Store and Cineplex challenge the conventional blank envelopes which typify these buildings and explore new ways for them to connect to an urban context. In order to produce a unique experience for both visitors and those passing by, and to make the building unique to Leicester, a number of cultural and historical references have been used to animate the block and enrich the retail and leisure experience.

John Lewis Department Store

Department stores are conventionally designed as blank enclosures to allow retailers the flexibility to rearrange their interior layouts. However, the physical experience of shops is an increasingly important consideration to compliment the convenience of online shopping. The concept for the John Lewis store is a net curtain, providing privacy to the interior without blocking natural light.

The design of the store provides the retail flexibility required without removing the urban experience from shopping. The store cladding is designed as a double glazed façade with a pattern introduced, making it like a net curtain. This allows for a controlled transparency between the store interiors and the city, allowing views of the exterior and natural light to penetrate the retail floors whilst also future-proofing the store towards changes in layout. Thus, the store is able to reconfigure its interiors without compromising on its exterior appearance.

FOA's pattern design introduces a number of local references from Leicester and John Lewis to a pattern selected from John Lewis's archive of textile patterns. The use of pattern draws inspiration from Leicester's 200 years of textiles and weaving, the translucency of saris worn by the Indian population living in Leicester and John Lewis' own tradition of producing quality fabrics.

The pattern itself is formed of four panels of varying density which allow for a variable degree of transparency. These meet seamlessly across the perimeter, producing a textile-like cladding. Fritted in mirror onto two layers of glass curtain wall, the mirrored pattern reflects its surroundings and in doing so becomes further integrated into its context, densifying and changing as the sun moves around the building. Viewed frontally from the retail floors, the double façade aligns to allow views out, whilst an oblique view from street level displaces the two patterns and creates a moiré effect, reducing visibility and increasing visual complexity, thereby maximising the privacy performance.

Cineplex

In order to establish a consistent identity between the cinema and department store, the curtain concept is extended to the cinema. This curtain both associates the cinema and department store and resonates with the theatre curtains which were a traditional interior feature of cinemas. Cineplexes are usually large volumes containing multiple screens which require no daylight in the interiors, except in the lobby areas. To cater for the twelve cinema screens it encloses, the Leicester Cineplex needs to be equally opaque and therefore, its curtain is designed as an opaque stainless steel rain screen. In order to enliven this curtain, the stainless steel façade is treated in mirror finish and pleated at different scales to diffuse the large volume into a series of smaller reflective surfaces.

Awarded:

2009 RIBA Award

The RIBA (Royal Institute of British Architects) International Awards reward the excellent work being done by RIBA members around the world. The shortlisted projects for the Lubetkin Prize are chosen from the winners of the RIBA International Awards.

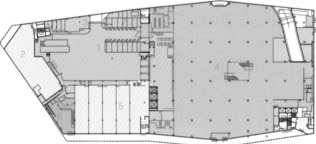

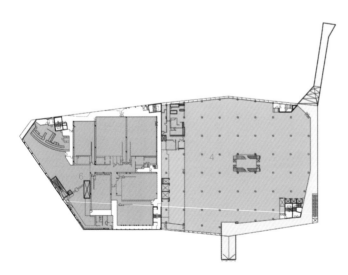

1. Service yard
2. Retail
3. Services
4. Department store
5. Retail units
6. Cinema
7. Vaughan way

Jinso Pavilion

Designer: Cepezed Architects /Jan Pesman, Hans Cool, Joost Heijnis, Bart van Lieshout **Location:** Amsterdam, The Netherlands **Completion date:** 2008 **Photographer:** Fas Keuzenkamp

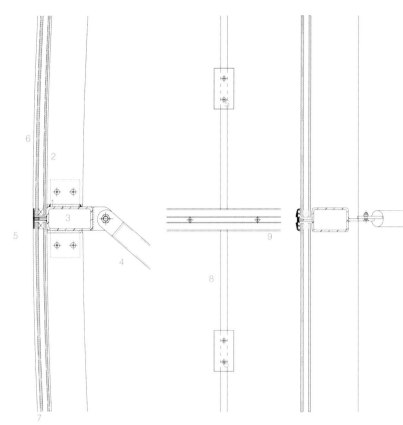

1. Profiles welded on all sides for the mounting of the hot-rolled and cold-shaped steel rails; on the top, they are fastened with flanged bolts provided with an inner hexagon
2. Bent horizontal box rails in colour NCS S 8000-N
3. Vertical steel girders in colour NCS S 8000-N
4. Tie rods and compression bars Ø 48, 3, 5 mm in colour NCS S 8000-N
5. Vertically, the glass is clamped with metal plates in colour NCS S 8000-N
6. Cold-bent freeform insulation glass
7. Horizontally fully clamped with black muffled aluminium extrusion profile
8. All vertical joints are sealed with black cement
9. The aluminium extrusion profile is mounted with countersinked tap screws provided with inner hexagon in the colour of the profile

The brand-new Jinso Pavilion is the extension to an Asian food catering pavilion that the Delft-based Cepezed Architects already built in the 1990s. Due to the scale enlargement of the entire area during the last decade, the Municipality of Amsterdam requested the owner and operator to invest in high-quality expansion. Cepezed was called for again.

The original building consists of an elongated, two-storey box measuring twenty by eight metres. In the initial enlargement designs, the extension involved a skin of ETFE cushions that constituted a roofed-over winter garden, stretching over the pavilion as a kind of rotation figure. As a result of various regulations and a refinement of the programme by the client, the concept eventually evolved into a transparent glass oval, more than twelve metres high and measuring forty-three by thirty metres in length and width, accommodating wholly climatised bar and restaurant functions. On the ground floor, the main volume has a two-metre constriction, while the first floor has a gallery more than four metres wide.

The façade and the roof are particularly striking. The façade consists of cold-bent insulation glass, which was bent and placed by means of suckers on the site itself. On the ground floor, the façade can be opened over more than three quarters of its length by means of a facetted folding wall in which every separate part has a different radius. The façade accommodates three stability crosses, of which two are situated at the heads of the oval. These locations are also used for the organisation of the stairs.

The roof is more than 2.5 metres high and comprises eight large pneumatic cushions of 4.20 metres wide, mounted on a refined detailed steel construction of facetted deltabeams. Each of the cushions consists of four layers of EFTE with three air chambers in each cushion. The EFTE bears a pattern through which the sun and light resistance can be regulated by a change in pressure in the innermost chamber. The air supply for the cushions is integrated in the construction.

A cooling patio has been integrated in the roof for the building-related installations that must have contact with the outside world. Embedded in large plant pots that were cast in the floor at the time of construction, the greenery appears natural and self-evident. The construction also contains two spaces of respectively forty-seven and seventy-four square metres that are lettable to other (catering) enterprises.

Awarded:

2008 Amsterdam Architecture Prize Nomination
Jinso was nominated for the Amsterdam Architecture Prize (A.A.P.), a yearly architecture award for a newly realised building within the city limits. The jury aims to award the building that is either the most beautiful, the most challenging and innovative or the most illustrative for the contemporary Amsterdam situation as a whole.

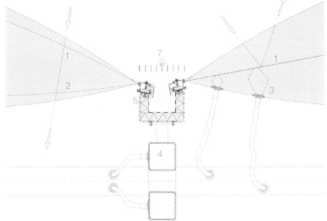

1. Four-layered EFTE air cushion with which the daylight incidence can be controlled. For the purpose of water return, the cushion has a flange to it which is fixed with a locking clamp of aluminium and rubber.
2. Open situation
3. Closed situation
4. Air-transporting steel rail profile of the convex beam; complete steel construction in colour NCS S 8000-N
5. Multifaceted gutter of set steelplate on convex beam; EPDM gutter coating glued to high quality insulation
6. Mounting profile of aluminium and rubber, having connection with gutter coating through glued seam and welded flap
7. Gratings that can be walked on, mounted on supports welded to the gutter bottom and equipped with leashing facilities

Left: Interior views of the restaurant on the ground floor
Right: Interior view of the restaurant on the first floor

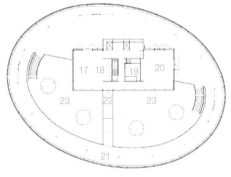

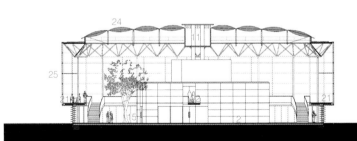

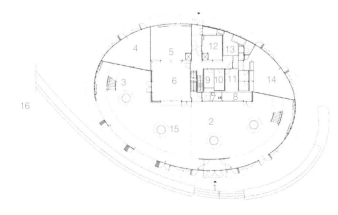

1. Entrance
2. Restaurant
3. Staircase
4. Area for rent
5. Kitchen
6. Take-out/Distribution point
7. Toilet for disabled
8. Storeroom
9. Freezing chamber
10. Cold store
11. Installations room
12. Dish washing kitchen
13. Transformer room
14. Area for rent
15. Tree box
16. Sidewalk terrace
17. Buffet
18. Kitchen
19. Storeroom
20. Restaurant lounge
21. Gallery/Restaurant
22. Overhead bridge
23. Void
24. Four-Layer EFTE Air Cushions
25. Cold-bent Insulation Glass

Scandinavian Golf Club

Designer: Henning Larsen Architects **Location:** Farum, Denmark **Completion date:** 2010 **Photographer:** Thorbjoern Hansen

With its location in the beautiful, hilly landscape of the previous training area of Farum military barracks, the Scandinavian Golf Club comprises an exclusive nature park and golf course of 2 x 18 holes.

The architectural vision has been to bridge the gap between the traditional American golf club and the functional architecture of Scandinavia. The golf club is a traditional wing house but is built in rustic materials with large cantilevers and oblique angles. The roof floats above the plateau as a sculptural element integrated in the hilly landscape, tree crowns and clouds of the sky.

The fine, sophisticated materials and exquisite craftsmanship provide the building with a high degree of exclusivity and ensure a unique balance between the architecture and the surrounding landscape. The extensive use of the wood species Douglas, Norwegian slate, stone and tombac combined with the generous inflow of daylight through the large windows provide the building with a weighty yet light expression.

The project won the Annual Award of the Copenhagen Carpenters' Guild in 2009, which is presented by the Copenhagen Carpenters' Guild. The president of the award committee, guild master of the Copenhagen Carpenters' Guild Flemming Kjærgaard, stated this reason for the committee's choice: "Headed by Soren Ollgaard, Henning Larsen Architects has designed a masterpiece that is in the field between Frank Lloyd Wright's significant houses and functional Scandinavian architecture. With its large cantilevers, courageous lines and a combination of few but high-quality materials, the clubhouse is a pleasure to look at and stay in."

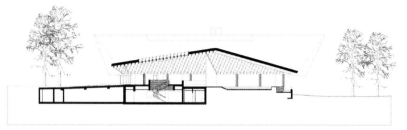

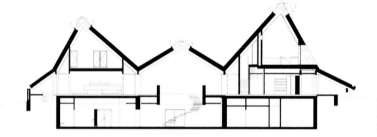

Right: The sculptural roof

Awarded:
2009 Annual Award of the Copenhagen Carpenters' Guild

Left: The vision balance between the function and the form
Top right: Materials ensure a unique balance between the architecture and the surrounding landscape
Bottom right: Norwegian slate

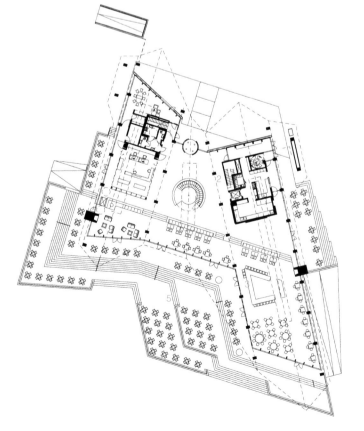

1. Toilet
2. Dressing room
3. Bar
4. Stairs
5. Dining area

Casa Club Bosque Altozano

Designer: Parque Humano **Location:** Morelia, Mexico **Completion date:** 2009 **Photographer:** Paul Rivera / ArchPhoto

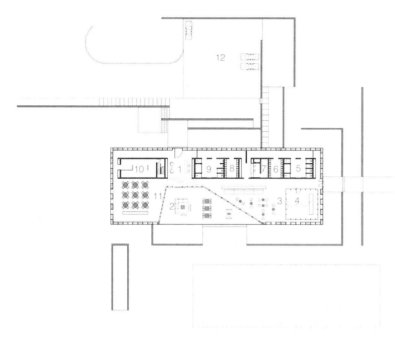

1. Lobby
2. Terrace
3. Lounge
4. Shop
5. Restroom
6. Dressing room
7. Control
8. Dressing room
9. Restroom
10. Kitchen
11. Restaurant
12. Motor lobby

Top right: South-east elevation
Bottom right: South-west elevation

The site is located in the Golf Course of Bosque Altozano in Morelia, Mich, Mexico. It faces to the south and east the mountain valley of Montaña Monarca (rich in a variety of pine and oak trees). Temperature reaches a 28°C in summer and 6°C in winter.

The programme of the project includes: restaurant, kitchen, open terrace, living space, golf shop, bath and dressing room.

The building occupies a natural ledge on a hillside looking towards the panoramic valley of Montaña Monarca in Morelia, Mexico. The building has been conceived as a homogenous stone mass, hollowing out a huge opening that slopes from ceiling to floor, framing the hillside panorama. A sloped celosia grid meant to evoke renaissance perspective drawings was placed in the middle of the core in order to distort and emphasise the view.

The amber light filtering through the artisanal stained glass placed on the celosia window blends with the coloured space, generating a chromatic continuity that during the course of the day moves imperceptibly through an endless scale of oranges, reds and yellows. Light also enters through two wooden skylights located in the middle of the room, helping to balance the coloured light that comes from the window.

A few rich, tactile materials were used in combination with the light to create a strong ambiance. Apart from the timber on the roof, the house consists of a steel frame covered by local stone, all recovered from the infrastructure works. The programme inside the house consists of a dining space, an open terrace, a lounge area, dressing room and kitchen.

The building resides effortlessly on a soft slope with privileged views absorbed by the wide-open façade that frames the natural panorama with an inviting forced perspective effect caused by the asymmetric glassed walls of the foyer. Lounge area, dining space and an open terrace are the interior programme.

Ceramic, amber and terracotta shades dominate the surfaces blending the house with the surroundings. This effect is granted by local stone used on the walls and floors, covering the steel structure. Timber roof and other wooden materials on the inside confirm the elegant and masculine appeal. That's Mexico alright.

Awarded:

2010 XI Biennial of Mexican Architecture / Silver Medal

The XI Biennial of Mexican Architecture identifies the best architectural works of the country as well as publications, research and theses; recognising its authors and spreading the most important works to allow, through analysis and critical opinion, a reflection on contemporary architecture. Participation in the Biennale was directed to those built works, research, publications, theses and academic projects conducted during the 2008-2010 biennium.

The jury was composed by renowned architects, academics and critics of architecture appointed by the Federation of Associations of Architects of the Mexican Republic (FCARM). Abstraction, the sustainable proposal, the way light works and the connection with the context made Casa Club Bosque Altozano win the silver medal in the category of "Recreation, Services, Sports and Landscape Architecture".

Top right: Main entrance
Bottom right: North-east elevation

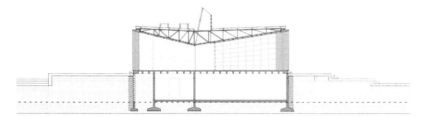

Top left: Open terrace
Bottom left: Interior view
Right: Corridor

Neiman Marcus at Natick Collection

Designer: Elkus Manfredi Architects **Location:** Massachusetts, USA **Completion date:** 2007
Photographer: Bruce Martin

The Neiman Marcus specialty shop in Natick is the most unusual and unique shop for a company whose corporate policy prescribes that each store be tailored to its business location. Furthermore, Neiman Marcus requires that the architecture respond to its primarily female customer base.

Elkus Manfredi Architects designed the undulating patterned stainless steel exterior of the shop to evoke a sophisticated silk dress or scarf from the Neiman Marcus couture line billowing in the coastal breezes of New England. The surrounding landscape recalls the sea grass of tidal marshes, the traditional stone walls, and birch forests of the region.

The majority of the frontage is along Speen Street, which is a major vehicular link from downtown Natick to Interstate 90. The form and scale is driven by its location. The form creates large bellows for the entry and signage, and then condenses the folds along Speen Street to create a dramatic image.

The most striking element of the project is an undulating two-storey-high stainless steel exterior that is meant to represent a silk scarf or dress in multiple hues of bronze, champagne and silver. To create the image of the fabric, Elkus Manfredi explored not only the form but the colour, texture, and pattern of the façade. The colours of the metal are timeless — bronze, champagne, and silver. The pattern follows the form and enhances moments within the building, such as the entry and signage.

The interior of the shop is luxurious, in keeping with other NM specialty shops. Coordination of structural steel with multi-coloured architectural stainless steel panels was a major challenge.

Three-dimensional spatial coordinates were furnished in electronic format, and then the structural steel fabricator used this information to fabricate bearing seats. Proactive planning for the interface between the structural members and stainless steel panels meant that the different coloured ribbons appeared flawless.

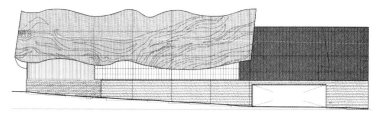

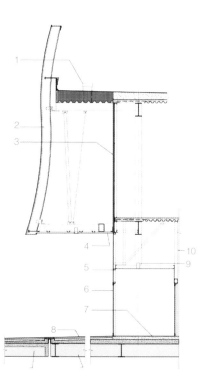

1. Roof vents for rain screen cavity
2. Metal rain screen
3. Metal panels
4. Stainless steel soffit panel
5. Glazed aluminium curtain wall
6. Stainless steel entrance doors
7. Entrance mat
8. Stone pavers
9. Lighting
10. Partition of entry vestibule

Right: Exit

Awarded:
Private Project of the Year, 2008
Construction Management Association of America, New England Chapter
Retail Store of the Year, 2007
Chain Store Age Magazine

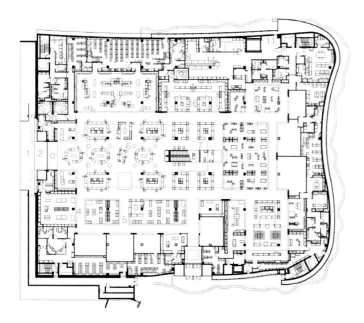

1. Mall exterior
2. Vestibule
3. Maison
4. Fashion accessories
5. Designer handbags
6. Cosmetics/fragrances
7. Design jewellery
8. Men's sportswear
9. Catering
10. Fitting rooms
11. Staging
12. Workroom
13. Office
14. Wrap/pack & delivery
15. Cash
16. Precious jewel
17. Ladies shoes
18. Communication room
19. Men's & women's
20. Cosmetic treatment

Top right: Side view
Bottom right: Façade detail

19 George Road

Designer: 3DReid **Location:** Edgbaston, UK **Completion date:** 2007 **Photographer:** Hufton & Crow

This relatively small, stand-alone office building near the city centre fits well within its surroundings despite the variation in style from neighbours. The scheme provides an exceptional public profile from the street and has created a strongly structured, finely stylised end product. Despite being on a tight site, the aspect out of the building is very good, providing high levels of natural light to public and private areas. Concentration on providing a mixed-mode ventilation system and achieving an excellent BREEAM rating is pleasing in an environment that might otherwise have been used for a more traditional building.

The 1,595-square-metre headquarters building tailored for Shaw Tax Limited but with the flexibility to sub-divide the two floors should the tenant decide to move on in the future.

The development is based on the concept of a "floating" office box set in a green landscaped clearing, and is centred round a private courtyard which provides a focus for the whole building. The tenant has demanded a design that both enhances their public profile from the street, while also preserving their privacy in what, architecturally, is otherwise a very traditional street in the leafy suburb of Edgbaston. Attention has been paid to creating a comfortable environment with an emphasis on quality and discipline rather than opulence.

The brief has demanded that the building be BCO 2005 compliant; have the capacity to cater for multiple tenancies; create 1,115 square metres of office floor space over two levels; provide adequate car parking provision and utilise mixed-mode ventilation.

Thin 500-millimetre-wide, full-height windows set to a 1,500-millimetre grid achieve an environmental solution that meets the new Part L2 regulations. This solution architecturally creates a varied façade, provides the required amount of daylight to give a good office space and is also economical.

The designers have designed a building that offers a confident expression of individuality and a modern identity. To give both a focus to the scheme and a positive "aspect" from the internal office environment, a generous internal courtyard has been created affording views into and beyond the space to take advantage of the wonderfully green Conservation Area setting. Absolutely key to the building are its "green" credentials and it has received an "Excellent" BREEAM rating, making it the first office building in Birmingham to achieve this environmental standard and recognition.

Right: The main entrance to the office building

Awarded:

2007 British Council of Offices Award: Best Small Project (Midlands & East Anglia Region)

Every year, the cream of UK corporate real estate gather to celebrate the very best in excellent office space at the BCO Awards. One of the BCO's primary objectives is to define excellence in office space. As part of this objective, the annual Awards Programme provides public recognition for top-quality design and functionality and a benchmark for excellence in workplaces. The Programme acknowledges innovation and focuses external attention on examples of best practice.

It is recognised that the opportunities and challenges set by each development are different and diverse. A key question for the judges will therefore be whether the applicant team has made the best of the circumstances presented to them. In making their assessment, the judges will, amongst other factors, assess:

- Project aims and rationale
- Utility of the product
- Specification and design solutions
- Quality of build
- Effectiveness of a workplace
- Enterprise and innovation
- Value, cost and programme
- Energy and sustainability
- Local context and impact
- Lifting the spirits

The key aspirations and brief have evidently paid off well, with full occupancy and a good level of positive feedback from the occupier. While the building lacks commercial flexibility, it has an exceptional "feel good" factor and the regional judges were unanimous in their decision in making the award. The national panel was impressed by the boldness of a major local landowner creating modern offices when it could have easily been made do with repeating the traditional vernacular. This will help set a tone for the shape of regeneration by rebranding what had become a tired estate. Construction was fast and of generally high quality, although let down by a few details. However, the exceptional speed in which the plans were approved showed a refreshing relationship of trust and understanding with local planners which bodes well for a shared vision for the future.

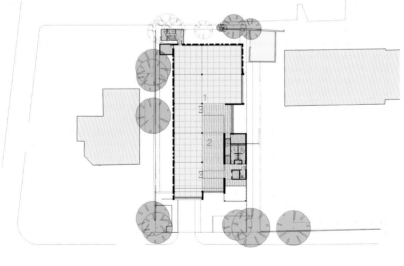

1. Working area
2. Reception area and recreational space
3. Washing room

Top left: Reception area and recreational space on the second floor
Bottom left: The staircase leading to the second floor

Top right: Atrium of the office building
Bottom right: The open working area

Harley Davidson Headquarters

Designer: Tony Owen NDM Architects **Location:** Sydney, Australia **Completion date:** 2005
Photographer: Brett Boardman

Sydney Architects Tony Owen NDM have designed the new Australian headquarters Harley Davidson. The building is located in Lane Cove and forms an iconic gateway to the new Lane Cove River business park.

For design inspiration they looked to the bikes themselves; their emotion and efficiency. The geometry of the engines forks and frames can be seen in the lines of the building. The building does not copy them, however, it suggests this movement and style. Rather than use the shape literally, they sought to express the elegance and aerodynamics of this movement in the lines of the building.

The brief for the building was a strong reflection of the Harley Davidson culture. The designers gave as much emphasis to the gymnasium and break-out areas as the office and storage space. The building is designed to reflect this. The designers located all of the recreational and break-out areas near the entry. You enter into a central mezzanine. From there you can see all of the areas that reflect the Harley lifestyle: the showroom, café, library, even the Gym. You are immediately aware of what Harley Davidson is all about. The building is designed so that, from the entry, you can also look down into the technical workshops and training areas. In this way you get a sense of the technical aspects of the company. It was important not to lose sight of the grungy side of the motor cycles as well.

The facility contains administrative offices, technical training and storage facilities for the iconic motorcycle company. The landmark building will form the striking centrepiece for a new high-tech business park on the Lane Cove River, developed by Demian Developments Pty Ltd.

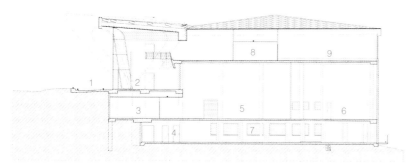

1. Footpath
2. Entry
3. Technical
4. Kitchen
5. Workshop area
6. Trailer exit
7. Staff parking
8. Toilet
9. Open office space

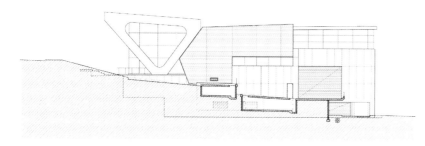

Awarded:

2009 Best Commercial/Industrial Project in the CNBC Asia Pacific Property Awards

The designers of Tony Owen NDM thought to design a building that reflects the uniqueness of Harley Davidson. HD is not simply a brand; for many it is an entire lifestyle and attitude. HD has a unique philosophy; it is at once about the expression of function and beauty through pure design, but it is also about freedom: the freedom of self expression and the freedom of the open road. This image is closely related; it is about good design, but also about challenging the norm. The designers designed a building that expressed this freedom and speed.

Right: Entrance

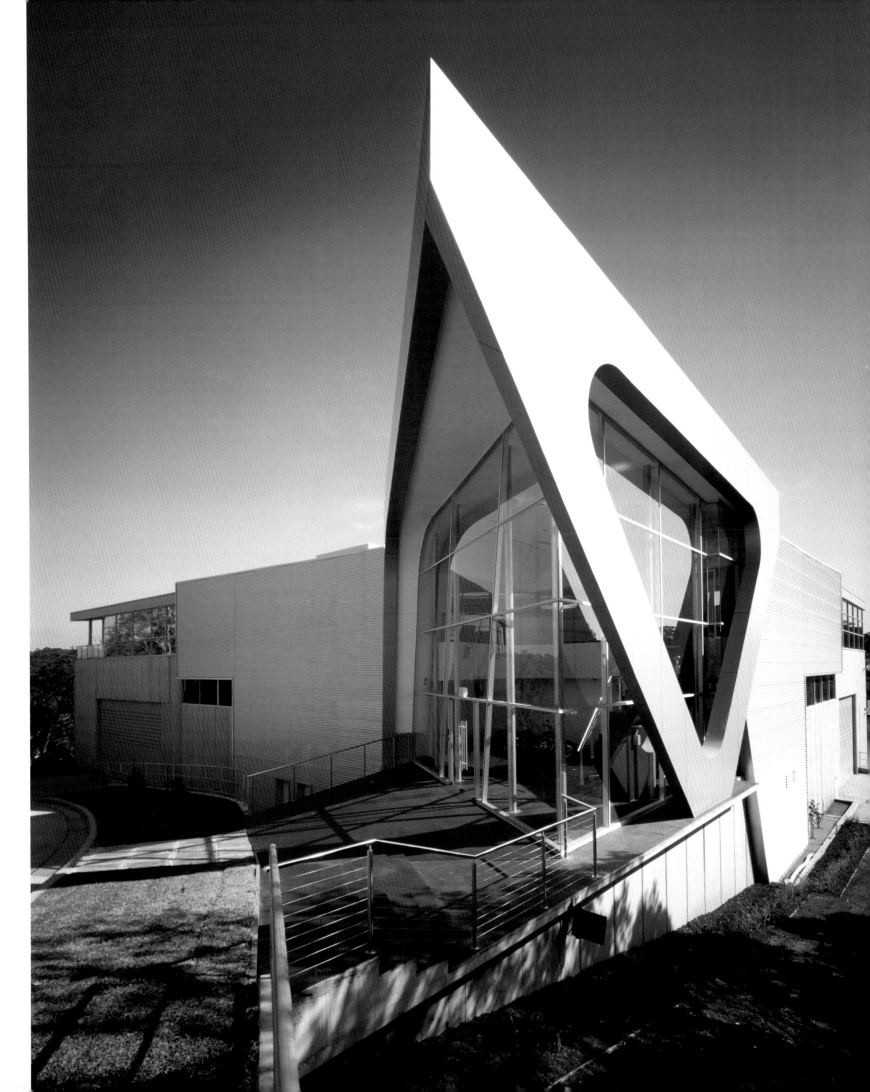

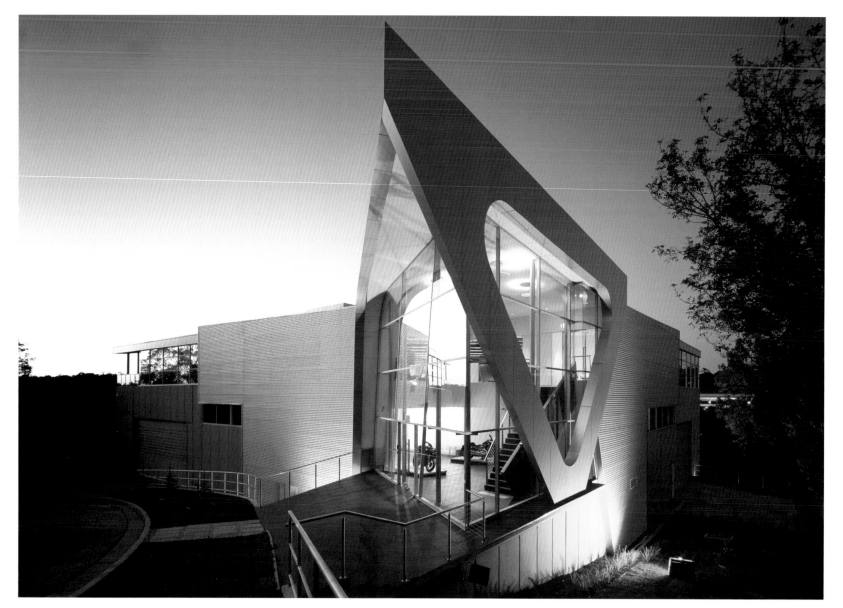

Left: Lighting at night

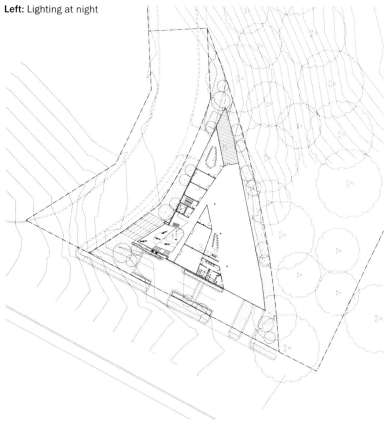

1. Entrance
2. Kitchen
3. Workshop area
4. Meeting room
5. Terrace

Oklahoma City Federal Building

Designer: Ross Barney Architects **Location:** Oklahoma City, Oklahoma, US **Completion date:** 2004
Photographer: Ross Barney Architects

This new facility is about the future, seeking to reunite the federal community and stands as a symbol of freedom.

The design of the new Federal Building in Oklahoma City maximised sustainable design and workplace productivity initiatives. Most expanses of curtain wall in the building are oriented to the north, northeast, or northwest and have horizontal shading elements to limit the impact of western summer sun and redirect daylight onto interior ceiling surfaces. The southeast-facing curtain wall is protected with a combination of shading elements and a deep roof overhang. The building was designed to receive an LEED Silver rating.

The floor plate is shaped similar to a traditional U-shaped building plan. This provides natural day lighting and vistas for each employee. Horizontal shading devices and Low E glazing shield the interior from solar heat gain. Horizontal shading devices are constructed of white awning material to not only shade the glazing below them but to redirect much of the incident sunlight onto the interior ceiling surface to enhance day lighting.

Awarded:
2006 General Services Administration Design Award
2005 Interior Architecture Award, AIA Chicago
2005 Divine Detail Award, AIA Chicago
2004 Sustainable Design Award, AIA Chicago
2003 Excellence in Construction Award, Associated Builders and Contractors

The project of Oklahoma City Federal Building was awarded for the following reasons:
· Iconic Design
· Level IV Federal Security Design Criteria
· Cost Effective/Innovative Design $185/sf
· Mends urban fabric
· Designed for LEED Silver criteria
· Blend of Openness and Security
· GSA Art in Architecture programme
· Designed with input from victims of terrorist attack

Right: Light coloured roofing materials were specified

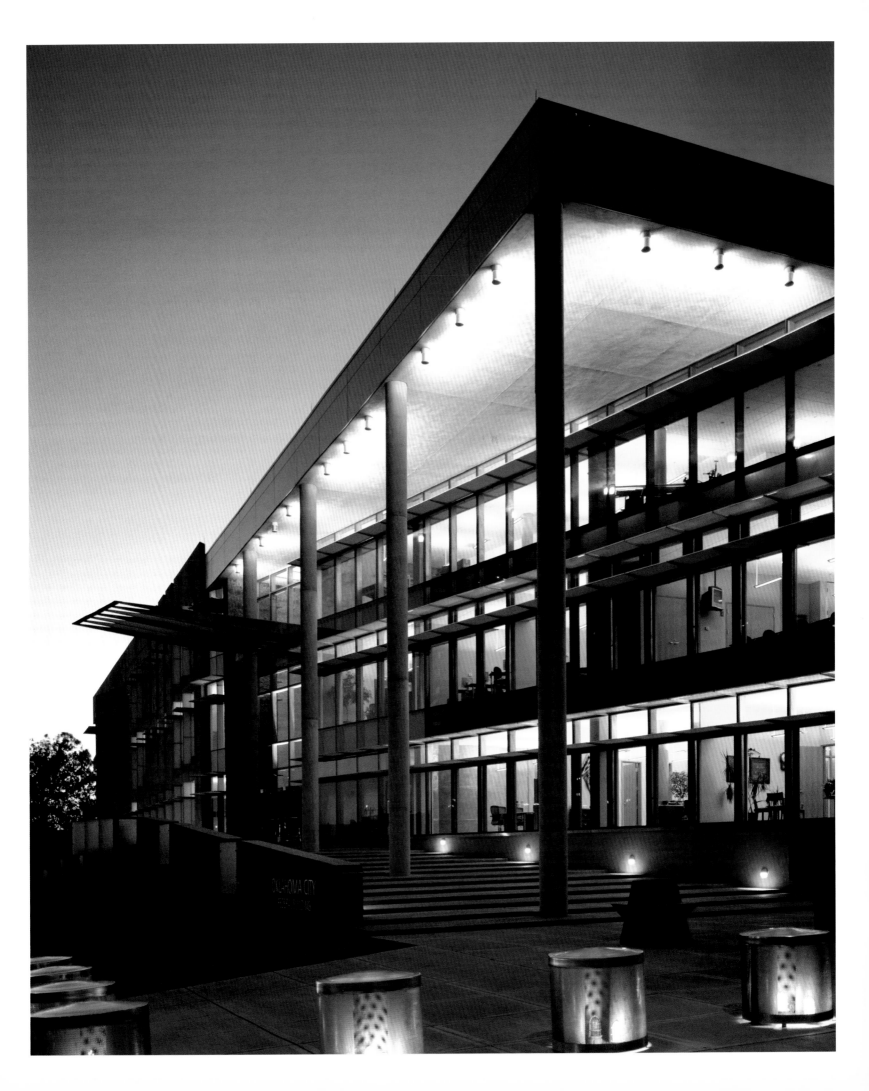

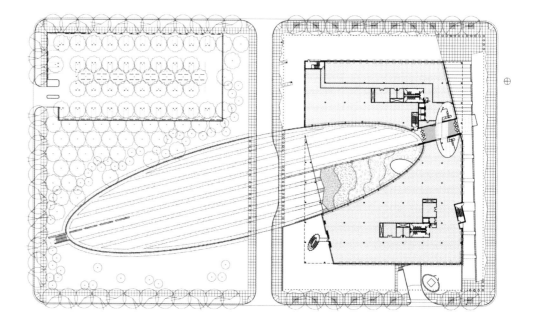

Top right: Glazing has been designed to utilise daylighting
Bottom right: The floor plate is shaped similar to a traditional U-shaped building plan with the goal that no workstation be more than 59'-0" from exterior glazing.

Rubner Haus AG Headquarters

Designer: Gerd Bergmeister Architekten & Baukraft architektur **Location:** Kiens, Italy **Completion date:** 2006 **Photographer:** Jürgen Eheim, Hertha Hurnaus

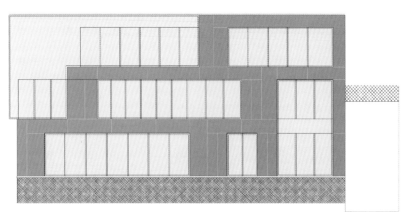

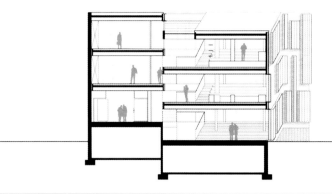

The path that leads from the concept for a commercial property to a complete building is usually a long one and consequently involves considerable expenditure in terms of both time and money. In erecting its own company building, the Rubner Haus AG was able to shorten this path by exploiting the advantages offered by systemised timber building. In only nine months the plans by architect Gerd Bergmeister and Baukraft (Georg Rubner and Dominik Rieder) were translated into a modern office building with a gross floor area of 2,300 square metres.

With its conspicuously styled façade, the cladding made of black larch wood, and the irregular, overhanging window boxes, which are in rhythm with the building's outer skin, the building calls attention to itself. The matt black colouring achieves a refinement of the material, which along with the large incisions into the façade confers the building an expression of strength and a monolithic character.

The cone-shaped building narrows towards the southerly direction, enabling an optimum natural lighting of the offices facing East and West. A preexisting step in the terrain demanded a split-level construction; this confers the building additional dynamism and helps easing its rigour.

The window boxes of differing sizes enable insights, regardless of the internal room functions and storeys. Furthermore, they break the rigorous geometry of this functional construction. The company logo was integrated quasi as an architectonic symbol, and due to its colouring it is widely visible in the landscape.

Unlike its compact outer skin, the inside of the building is marked by transparent permeability. The contrasting characters of outside and inside, dark and bright, matt and shiny, massive and delicate are part of the overall concept. The building opens itself to unexpected visual perspectives. The inside is characterised by an open layout while the interiors are marked by exciting perspectives.

The headquarters of the Rubner Haus AG was designed as a large passive energy building, which complies with the strictest criteria as regards sustainable use of energy: the annual heating requirements are only $7kWh/m^3$, with a gross floor area of 2,300 square metres that is around 1,300 litres of heating oil per year. An exhaust and supply ventilation system with a rotation heat exchanger as well as a conventional underfloor heating system that uses wood left over from the production help to reduce the consumption of energy. And this in turn means – especially in buildings with a large floor area – an enormous saving in costs. Furthermore, it means that the building has an excellent ecological balance and shows that today it is indeed possible to erect environmentally-friendly buildings with large volumes.

Awarded:

2006 Best Climate House

Gerd Bergmeister and baukraft (Dominik Rieder and Georg Rubner) are the recipients of the 2006 Best Climate House for their planning of the new Rubner Company Headquarters office building.

Fossil fuel sources are becoming more and more limited, a fact which cannot be denied. Whoever would like to live comfortably, without making compromises, must therefore consider alternatives. Energy waste can be limited by use of renewable energy sources, foresight in planning and lasting construction techniques.

Construction of homes has always been an important economic engine, and investments in this field have positive effects in the entire economy. The KlimaHaus Agency has the goal of fusing ecological activity with economic thinking. A home with a high quality of life does not have to be expensive – on the contrary, it offers a range of opportunities both to save money and to protect the environment.

The KlimaHaus Agency supports the construction of energy-saving buildings and awards every year the best examples out of the categories living, working, tourism, energy plus and renovation.

The office building is characterised by a high standard of energy efficiency and a comfortable working environment. It reflects the philosophy of a company engaged in the production of energy saving buildings ("Climate House").

With this energy-saving and at the same time purposeful building, the company Rubner demonstrates its pioneering role in multiple aspects. The high-quality timber construction was chosen out of convincement and follows the company's philosophy of working predominantly with wood. One of the main concerns was the creation of an ideal indoor climate to make employees and customers feel at ease. A minimised energy input during the construction period and the short duration of this – only six months passed from the demolition of the preexisting building to the moving in – were the targets, as well as the utilisation of ecological building materials and a modern design. The completed building shows that all these requirements could be successfully accommodated.

Left: The high-quality timber construction was chosen
Right: Indoor climate to make employees and customers feel at ease

Walden Studios

Designer: Jensen Architects / Jensen & Macy **Location:** Geyserville, CA, USA **Completion date:** 2007
Photographer: Richard Barnes, Marion Brenner, Jack Journey

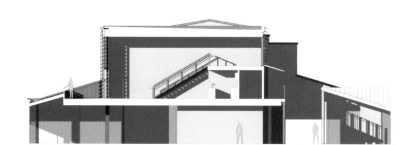

An existing concrete barn located on an agricultural site in Sonoma County. The structurally unsound wood frame roof of the barn was removed leaving only the existing perimeter concrete walls. The site has a railroad line on one side and open vineyards on the other.

The project consists of 1,245 square metres of mixed-use spaces, including commercial office space on the ground floor and work-live spaces on the upper floors. The Client requested flexible open plan spaces with views to the surrounding landscape. The strategy was to insert a new glass building inside the existing concrete walls.

The glass walls consist of a frameless structural glass fin system suspended from the roof and wrapping three sides of the building. The construction materials include mirror-like exposed concrete obtained with the use of plastic form liners; custom Italian stucco at existing walls; large insulated glass units, some with ceramic frit pattern; exposed burnished finish aluminum access floor system on raised pedestals; reclaimed cider barrel oak strip flooring clads the entire ceiling of the upper floors.

All building systems are distributed underneath a raised access floor system so that the structural concrete floor plate can be left exposed at the ceiling of the ground floor. Sustainability: a ground source (geothermal) heating and cooling system is located under the adjacent parking lot.

A gravel breezeway is cut all the way through the interior of the building. With full-height glass walls on both sides, this space brings the landscape into the building. The structure sits on a plinth raised above the floodplain of the Russian River. This plinth is landscaped with reflecting pools, olive and fruit trees, and looks out over rows of vineyards.

Awarded:
2008 ASLA Professional Awards – Honour Award for General Design
2008 AIA Redwood Empire Design Awards – Citation for Design
The American Society of Landscape Architects (ASLA) is an organisation based in Washington, DC. The Society's mission is to lead, to educate, and to participate in the careful stewardship, wise planning, and artful design of our cultural and natural environments.

Right: A new glass building was inserted inside the existing concrete walls

Right: Mirror-like exposed concrete obtained with the use of plastic form liners

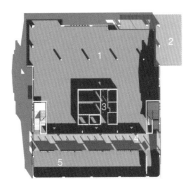

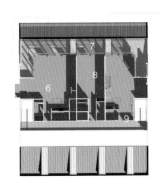

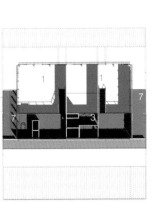

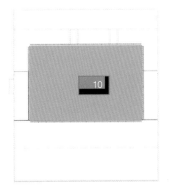

1. Studios
2. Reflecting pool
3. Core
4. Exterior court
5. Gallery
6. Art foundation
7. Terrace
8. Studios
9. Exterior balcony
10. Mechanical

Paju Book City

Designer: Stan Allen Architects **Location:** Paju, South Korea **Completion date:** 2009 **Photographer:** Stan Allen Architects

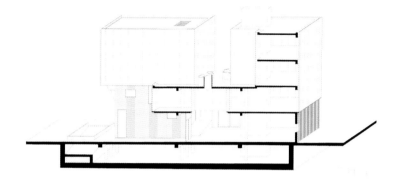

New York practice Stan Allen Architects has completed a building for the publishing industry in South Korea. Part of a development called Paju Book City, the building has an L-shaped plan that allows for a courtyard at the entrance. Book City is located in the Paju area, viewed as the "land of promise". Located just 30 kilometres from Seoul, it is a publishing cultural community conveniently located near the Jayu highway. From the beginning, the Book City project was planned and established as an industrial city related specifically to books. It is intended as a place devoted to planning, producing and distributing books by well-intentioned publishers.

The design features a roof garden and sliding shades behind the glass façade. Paju Book City is a 125-hectare "Urban Wetland" developed for the publishing industry in South Korea. SAA/Stan Allen Architects is one among a select group of foreign architects invited to design individual buildings within this innovative master plan. The project extends and elaborates the given "bookshelf typology" with an L-shaped volume that creates an entry court and an upper-level landscaped garden. The client is a young web publishing company looking for light, open and interconnected workspaces.

This simple L-shaped volume serves as a counterpoint to the highly active volumes of the other buildings within the complex, and is activated by the figure of the stairs moving up the elevation, exposing the rough stone base below. Behind the first layer of glass, a sliding panel system controls sunlight, creates privacy and creates a changeable pattern that is the counterpoint to the standardised curtain-wall system. This thick, responsive curtain-wall system is designed to moderate heat gain while activating the interior spaces.

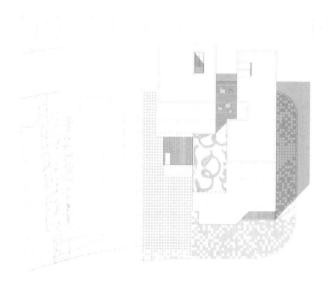

Awarded:

2009 AIA NY Architecture Honour Award
AIA New York's annual Design Awards Programme recognises outstanding architectural design by New York City architects and for work in New York City. The purpose of the awards programme is to honour the architects, clients, and consultants who work together to achieve design excellence.

Right: Street view

Top Left: Back view
Bottom Left: Street elevation
Right: Entry view and roof garden

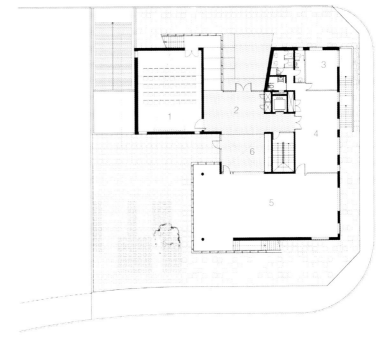

1. Lecture hall
2. Entrance
3. Reading room
4. Meeting room
5. Workspace
6. Display

Pall Italia Headquarters

Designer: Progetto CMR - Massimo Roj Architects **Location:** Milan, Italy **Completion date:** 2007
Photographer: Matteo Piazza & Angelo Gilardelli

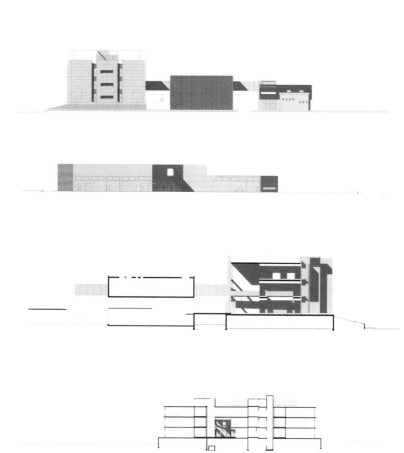

Under the distributive profile, the new Pall Italia site is divided into three buildings, two of which are newly built (buildings A and B), while a third (building C) was rebuilt from a pre-existing structure. Functional continuity is ensured by an overhead glass walkway, which links the first floors of the three units.

Building A, intended for offices and business visits, was the one which offered Progetto CMR the greatest opportunities for experimentation. Designed like a box with three solid sides (east, west and ceiling) and two sides made of glass (north and south), at night it turns into a sort of "urban lantern".

The three-storey Building A is built on three floors. The ground floor, besides housing specific areas for the reception of visitors, dedicates the entire western wing to meeting and conference rooms. From an aesthetic and formal point of view, the area of greatest prestige and importance is represented by the triple-height access area floored in Santafiora, which contains the panoramic lift as well as an elegant staircase in reinforced concrete, steel and glass.

It is, however, in the office area that the designers could fully express the long experience, acquired over the years, related to well being and quality of life in work spaces. Such experience leads to emphasising essential requirements such as flexibility, the sensory approach with the materials and the building's internal environment, as well as the long-term development of the company.

Building B, which houses the laboratories and the Life Sciences department, is strongly characterised by an architectural skin made up of transparent polycarbonate. This choice arises from a functional motivation, as well as from a desire to confer a greater visual dynamism to the building; in fact, this material can assume different colours and degrees of transparency depending on the external weather conditions.

Finally, Building C houses laboratories for the study of applications by Pall's industrial division, as well as smaller warehouses.

Awarded:

Finalist in 2008 ULI Awards for Excellence

ULI Awards for Excellence defines the standard for real estate development practice worldwide. In its 31st year, the awards programme is the centrepiece of ULI's efforts to identify and promote best practices in all types of real estate development. The awards recognise the full development process of a project – construction, economic viability, marketing, and management – as well as design.

Right: At night glass turns into a sort of "urban lantern" refined by the presence

The ULI Awards for Excellence honour development projects in three regions: the Americas, Europe, and Asia Pacific. Each region has its own jury, schedule, and fees. ULI – the Urban Land Institute is a nonprofit research and education organisation supported by its members. Founded in 1936, the institute now has more than 40,000 members worldwide representing the entire spectrum of land use and real estate development disciplines, working in private enterprise and public service.

As the preeminent, multidisciplinary real estate forum, ULI facilitates the open exchange of ideas, information and experience among local, national and international industry leaders and policy makers dedicated to creating better places. The mission of the Urban Land Institute is to provide leadership in the responsible use of land and in creating and sustaining thriving communities worldwide.

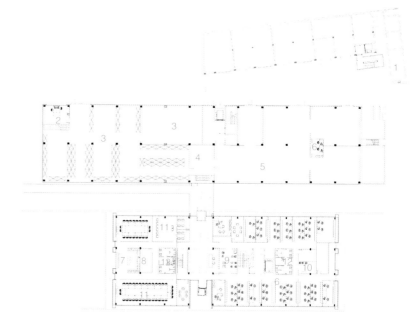

1. Waste room	7. Break room
2. Office/storage	8. Administration storage
3. Warehouse	9. Copy room
4. Equipment room	10. Printing room+archive
5. Workshop	11. Meeting room
6. Office	12. Toilet

Top right: The material can assume different colours and degrees of transparency depending on the external weather conditions

Left: Triple-height access area floored in Santafiora, which contains the panoramic lift as well as an elegant staircase in reinforced concrete, steel and glass

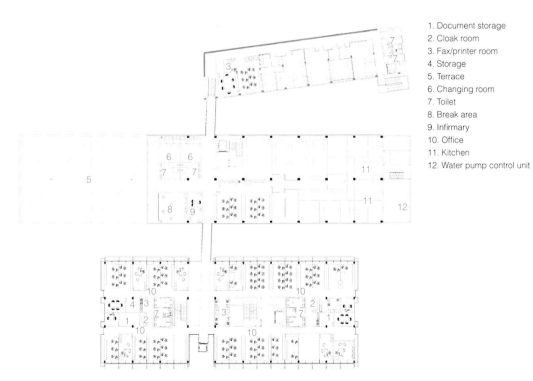

1. Document storage
2. Cloak room
3. Fax/printer room
4. Storage
5. Terrace
6. Changing room
7. Toilet
8. Break area
9. Infirmary
10. Office
11. Kitchen
12. Water pump control unit

Designer: Integrated Architecture / Michael C. Corby **Location:** Hudsonville, Michigan, USA **Completion date:** 2008 **Photographer:** Justin Maconochie

Lamar Construction Company Corporate Headquarters

It is not often that a company's identity can be literally expressed in its building. The corporate headquarters for this Construction Company, a premier general contractor which specialises in steel erection, formed concrete and pre-engineered buildings, does just that. The resolution of the design articulates who they are and what they do, eloquently proclaiming their skills and abilities to all who pass by on the nearby interstate highway.

The 4,830-square-metre hovering box of glass and steel celebrates their craft and long history of structural steel erection, showcasing their commitment to high quality construction efforts, no matter what the degree of difficulty is.

While the cantilever utilises raw space to create a powerful, essential building component, the headquarters project is simply one building with two volumes separated by a 5-metre gap. The solid, textured concrete tower grabs the glass box and gives it solid footing. The lower box, serves as a plinth with its primarily solid form and corporate hue completing this unique and bold expression of the floating box.

Even though the cantilever captures the eye, the remainder of the building serves an equally important role as it, too, and communicates the construction company's expertise. The simple 2,787-square-metre shop, a metal building, reflects their formidable experience in pre-engineered steel projects, as the company ranks first in the state and twenty-seventh in the nation in pre-engineered steel tonnage.

The simple intuitive purity of the building form didn't require a high-tech engineering approach, however though the innovative use of advanced computer vibration modelling and tuned mass damper technology, provided a backup plan that allowed the team to design closer to the edge of uncertainty without requiring the owner to pay for an overly conservative, expensive solution.

Field vibration testing took place throughout construction and tuned mass damper chambers were built into the floor, but the chambers remain empty and the damping devices were never ordered because the building performed without resorting to mechanical damping, exactly as anticipated. The mere availability of the technology, however, provided a safety net that allowed the designers to design simply and intuitively.

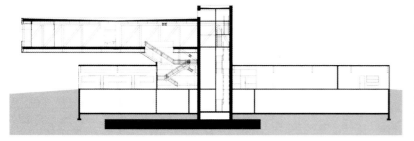

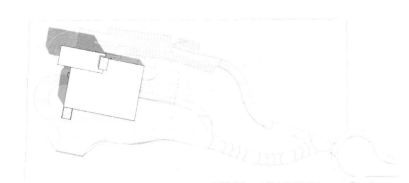

Right: The solid, textured concrete tower grabs the glass box and gives it solid footing

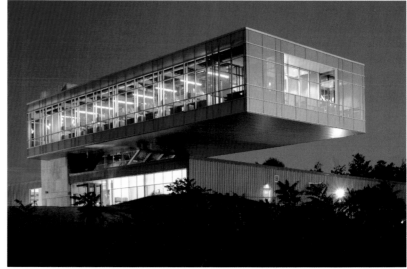

Awarded:

2009 International Design Award / Architecture / New Commercial Building / Third Place

2008 American Institute of Architects – Grand Valley Chapter

2008 American Institute of Architects – Michigan Chapter

Here are the comments from the jury: Unanimously picked by the jury as the project most deserving of recognition, this project was in a class of its own among the projects submitted; an amazing building; clean, dramatic, iconic, daring... a powerful statement of what the general contractor company owner stands for and is capable of; tectonically expressive of the materials... very well detailed; what an incredible truss! Working in that space, amongst that frame, must be awe-inspiring; the evening photos were very successful; graphically, the presentation of this project was the strongest of the submissions, a mark of a good project is when you almost can't take a "bad" picture of it. This project is an amazing representation of what the client does, not to mention the cantilever just blew us away.

"The International Design Awards remain focused on recognising visionary artists spanning all disciplines of design," said Hossein Farmani, the IDA founder, "We're thrilled to announce IDA's second season drawn in a record number of entries from almost twice as many countries as last year. The innovation and quality of this year's submissions have truly raised the bar for future competitions."

As much sculpture as building, this effort illustrates how simple, rectangular, linear forms can be arranged in a way that is anything but simple. A series of stacked, rectangular prisms and, the cantilever add dynamic energy creating an impressive demonstration of the laws of physics.

Right: The metal building reflects the architects' formidable experience in pre-engineered steel project

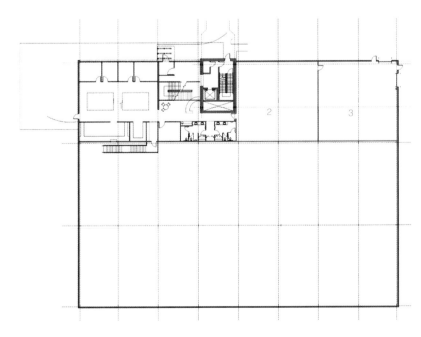

1. Office
2. Training
3. Wood shop

Kraton230

Designer: Mei Architecten en Stedenbouwers **Location:** Rotterdam, The Netherlands **Completion date:** 2007 **Photographer:** Jeroen Musch, Luuk Kramer

The building, which houses not only RTV Rijnmond but also other firms, forms the heart of the audio-visual sector in Rotterdam along with Schiecentrale. The sturdy character of the RTV Rijnmond building by Mei Architecten en Stedenbouwers, both in scale and appearance, is a direct reference to the large size of the Schiecentrale, a former electricity generating station, and to the imposing ships that used to dock on the quay nearby. The façade of the building is made of rusty brown cast-iron panels that are decorated with maritime and audio-visual motifs designed by Studio Job. The window openings in this cast-iron section extend over two levels. The ground-floor façade facing Lloydstraat is a transparent wall of glass below two cantilevered levels faced with steel panels. That gives this section of the building the character of a large awning that directs attention to the entrance and studios of RTV Rijnmond.

The entrance leads to a large hall containing studio spaces where regional radio and TV programmes are produced. Grouped around these studios are all the supporting spaces such as canteen, editorial spaces and server room. The studios hanging in the space and the big void give the setting the character of an industrial factory floor where news rather than harbour products is processed.

The two floors clad in metal panels are supported by two striking V-shaped stanchions whose tapering legs come together on the studio square. Spanning on top of the stanchions are two large lattice girders 45 metres in length. The whole setting has the character of a container crane placed indoors. Other structural elements also recall the industrial port activities of days gone by. The exposed sturdy bolt connections combine with the rusty façade to give the building a subtly well-used appearance.

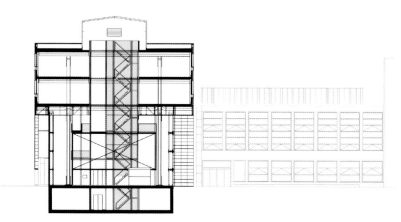

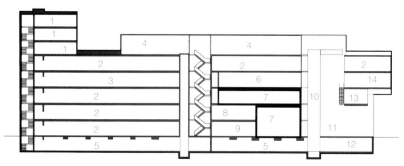

1. Atelier
2. Third parties
3. Offices RTVR
4. Installations
5. Parking
6. Edit
7. Studio
8. Car
9. Logistics
10. Lift shaft
11. Studio square
12. Storage
13. Management
14. Editorial office

Awarded:
Total Façade Architecture 2008: First Prize for Cast Iron Panels
National Steel Award 2008: Nomination
BNA building of the year 2008: Nomination
The Dutch Design Awards 2006: Selection

Right: The connection with the nearby situated Schiecentrale 4b

Top left: The interior of ARA defines itself by bright, transparent working areas
Bottom left: Big steel frameworks refer to the harbour architecture
Right: The ceiling of the walking bridge to the editorial room is embedded with concrete tiles

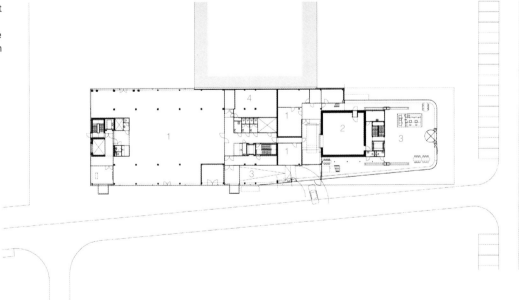

1. Offices
2. Other functions
3. Circulation
4. Storage

KINTEX

Designer: DeStefano + Partners **Location:** Goyang, South Korea **Completion date:** 2005 **Photographer:** Yong-Kwan Kim

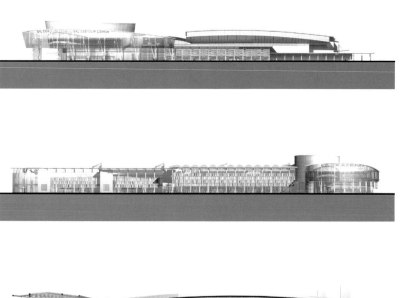

KINTEX is located in the city of Goyang, ideally situated halfway between the central city of Seoul and the New Incheon International Airport. The central spine through the convention complex's master plan connects the main entry of the convention centre with Goyang. Known as the "Garden City", Goyang is characterised by its lush floral gardens and parks. This identity is reinforced by the design of the convention centre with extensive landscaping that integrates the facility with the city and its park-like setting.

The glassy and colourful design concept dissolves the indoor/outdoor boundary and extends the landscaping indoors to a grand three-storey, skylit public pre-function space. The building's western exposure is characterised by a series of multi-coloured sunscreens which filter the light into the building and further enhance the natural qualities of the interior spaces.

With its strategic location on the Korean peninsula with land, sea and air access to worldwide markets, KINTEX is committed to attracting competitive exhibitions to strengthen South Korea's trade base and enhance the country's export competitiveness; it has become the leading exhibition facility in northeast Asia.

KINTEX is equipped with facilities and infrastructure superior to other exhibition centres all over the world. First, it has the largest exhibition area in South Korea. The first phase of construction created a facility equivalent in size to six football fields, attractive to large-scale international exhibitions. Second, it is built durable enough for large-size and/or heavy items. The floors of the exhibition centre are designed to endure five tons per square metre – perfect for displaying heavy and oversized equipment such as airplanes and large machinery. Third, KINTEX possesses high-tech devices and advanced exhibition techniques. Employing an Intelligent Building System (IBS), all the facilities in the centre are equipped with wireless LAN and web kiosks are also installed throughout so real-time exhibition and traffic information is available to visitors. With the best facilities, KINTEX is able to efficiently respond to the various demands of exhibition organiser and boost its reputation as an advanced international exhibition centre.

Completed in 2005, the first phase of a planned, four-phase complex is a 1.4 million-square-metre facility with a 54,997-square-metre pillar-free, open floor exhibition hall that is divisible into five smaller halls; 22 small- to medium-size meeting rooms, which may be combined or divided to provide breakout accommodations for exhibitions or independent conference venues; an oval, divisible grand ballroom that can seat up to 2,000; a VIP meeting room equipped for telecommunications and simultaneous translation in eight languages; outdoor exhibition space; food service and catering facilities; and other business amenities that support the convention centre's reputation as an international business plaza.

Top right: Ceremonial entrance with entry porte cochere

Awarded:
2006 Association of Licensed Architects (ALA) / Gold Medal & Presidential Award

KINTEX won the ALA Presidential Award and Gold Award for its innovative structure, good proportion, wonderful use of colour and bright sunny interior.

The project received these awards because of its outstanding architectural design, pleasing proportions, use of scale, sunny interior and contextual sensitivity to the surrounding residential community. The original master plan turned its back on the traditional low-rise housing neighbourhood to the north by locating the truck docks and services areas facing the historic district. As built, the architect rotated the building's orientation to hide the service and loading areas from the neighbourhood and create a low-rise entrance on the north to link the community to the complex and break down the scale of the large exhibition halls. The main façade is composed of several elements that serve to lighten the building's mass to a more human scale. Solid forms alternate with glassy areas and colourful sun-shading elements within a composition of light and airy pilotis to create a welcoming presence for this state-of-the-art facility.

Top left: Entrance hall
Top right: Entrance hall – trusses and skylights

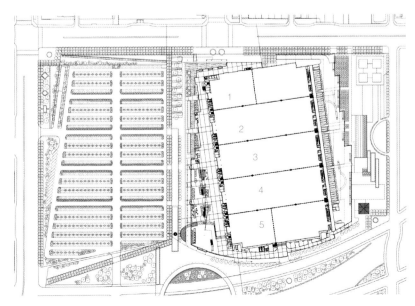

1-5. Hall

Colorado Convention Centre

Designer: Fentress Architects **Location:** Denver, Colorado, USA **Completion date:** 2004 **Photographer:** ©Scott Dressel-Martin, Ron Johnson, James P. Scholz, Nick Merrick © Hedrich Blessing

Building upon the success of the original convention centre, Fentress Architects forward-looking design offers efficient circulation, flexible meeting and exhibit space, and spacious, daylit interiors.

The massing, materials and rhythmic elements of the façades help integrate the structure into a downtown context enlivened by bustling pedestrian activity. Drawing the eye upward, a clean, crisp cantilever rising from Speer Boulevard, a main thoroughfare, is seen by nearly a million passersby annually. Day or night, the innovative glass and steel structure glows, accenting the 14th Street roof blades to create a striking and memorable identity. Rolling, perforated stainless steel panels articulate movement and animate the secondary entrances, meanwhile concealing loading docks and public parking – an innovative, cost-effective solution.

Graciously welcoming and orienting its visitors, the Convention Centre's lobbies are grand spaces reaching up to 30 metres high. A 244-metre-long, uninterrupted glass curtain wall – the span of an 80-storey building lying on its side – invites the Convention Centre's more than two million annual visitors to absorb panoramic views of the Rocky Mountains and downtown Denver. Via the curtain wall, the lobbies are suffused with daylight, accenting numerous pieces of city-commissioned public art complementary to the architecture. The soaring ceilings are detailed with curving metal panels and circular light fixtures that reflect classic modern style.

A wide corridor, or central spine, acts as a tour guide, with varied colour themes and patterns intuitively leading people to meeting destinations. The exhibit level offers nearly 55,740 square metres of contiguous exhibition space divisible into six individual halls. Similarly, 9,290 square metres of meeting space, two ballrooms totalling 7,897 square metres and a 5,000-seat auditorium can be configured into multiple smaller rooms. Event space extends outdoors with two terraces that offer extraordinary views of the mountains and downtown.

Located within blocks of Denver's finest downtown hotels, restaurants and the nine theatres in the Denver Performing Arts Complex, the Colorado Convention Centre has effectively served as a catalyst for significant economic growth and urban revitalisation. Some 427 linear metres of designated off-street, drop-off space surrounds the Convention Centre, weaving it into the urban fabric. So does the light rail station that runs through it, positioning the Convention Centre at the forefront of the region's emphasis on Transit Oriented Development. In 2005, the Convention Centre's net figures outperformed the budget by nearly USD $2 million dollars, while the expansion generated an additional USD $145 million in direct, indirect and associated spending; an additional USD $8 million in annual tax revenue; and nearly 9,000 new jobs for the local economy.

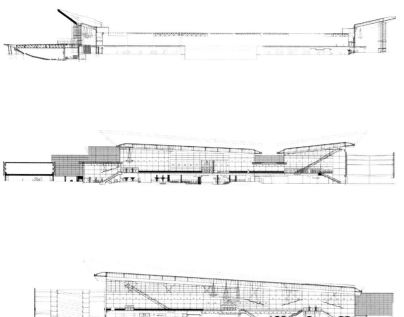

Right: A clean, crisp cantilever rising from Speer Boulevard, a main thoroughfare leading to downtown Denver

Awarded:

2008 American Architecture Award, Chicago Athenaeum/Metropolitan Arts Press with the European Centre for Architecture Design and Urban Studies

"The American Architecture Awards have become the foremost, prestigious awards programme for public recognition for Excellence in Architecture, both nationally and internationally. The Awards identify the new cutting-edge design direction, urban philosophy, design approach, style and intellectual substance in American Architecture today. "

Established over ten years ago, the awards recognise "the most significant new contemporary architecture, landscape architecture, interiors, and urban planning" by the "most renowned American and international design firms practicing in the U.S." Winning projects represent many U.S. states, but also Austria, Egypt, France, Kazakhstan, Korea, Kuwait, China and the United Arab Emirates. Only sixty-five awards were given out of hundreds of submissions.

Publicity includes an exhibit in Florence, Italy in November, 2008, organised by the Municipality of Florence and the Faculty of Architecture in Florence. After that, the exhibition travels to the European Centre's new Contemporary Art + Architecture Centre in Athens. In 2009, the exhibition started a national tour in the United States.

Top left: An 800-foot-long glass curtain wall
Bottom left: View of main pedestrian entrance, looking southwest
Right: Evening view of the pedestrian entrance

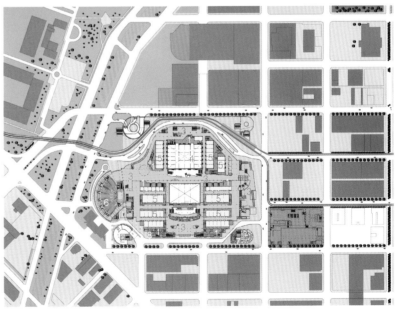

1. Admission
2. Hall
3. Conference room
4. Lobby
5. Void on lobby
6. Corridor
7. Archives department
8. Offices

Trade Fair Graz, Hall A

Designer: Riegler Riewe Architekten **Location:** Graz, Austria **Completion date:** 2008 **Photographer:** Riegler Riewe Architekten

The Graz trade fair grounds lie in a transitional zone between a dense urban residential area and a more relaxed, lower development to the south, interspersed with commercial use. With the construction of the Stadthalle, which was opened in 2002 and whose striking roof extends far into the street space, a symbolic building was created that establishes a sense of identity and takes up an important position in the urban context. In order not to impinge upon its striking independence and its visibility from the south, the new Hall 1 was not placed parallel but swivelled at an acute angle to the Stadthalle. The swivelled placing of the individual buildings results not only in an atmospherically varied urban situation but also makes it possible to create generously-sized approach, loading and open areas on the site.

Inside the two-storey hall we encounter a familiar theme: the spatial layering of function structures on a long axis. In this case, it is dense function strips allocated to the individual foyers that must be passed before entering the open hall itself. In addition, an element emerges that takes up the theme of transition between outside and inside: the hall has a double façade, and the space between its two layers accommodates the necessary escape stairs and lifts. While the inner, load-bearing walls are made of reinforced concrete, the outer façades consist of a curtain of expanded metal elements. This gives the hall a matt shimmering, silvery envelope that through its monochrome homogeneity differs clearly from the façade of the Stadthalle and, when required, can be used as a screen.

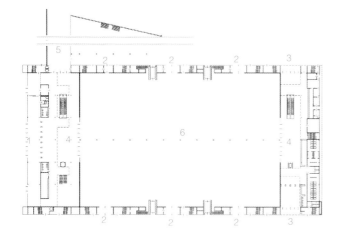

1. Main entrance
2. Entrance gates, delivery
3. Side entrance
4. Foyer
5. Passage to Convention Centre
6. Exhibition hall

Awarded:
2009 Nominee for the Mies van der Rohe Award
European Union Prize for Contemporary Architecture Mies van der Rohe Award is granted every two years by the European Union and the Fundació Mies van der Rohe, Barcelona, to acknowledge and reward quality architectural production in Europe.

In this way, the Award draws attention to the major contribution by European professionals to the development of new ideas and technologies. At the same time, it offers both individuals and public institutions an opportunity to reach a clearer understanding of the cultural role of architecture in the construction of our cities. Furthermore, the Award sets out to foster architecture in two significant ways: by stimulating greater circulation of professional architects throughout the entire European Union in response to transnational commissions and by supporting young architects as they set off on their careers.

Right: The outer façades consist of a curtain of expanded metal elements

The Award consists of a cash prize of 60,000 and a sculpture evoking Mies van der Rohe's German Pavilion. The Special Mention is endowed with 20,000€ and a sculpture evoking the Pavilion, the genuine symbol of the Award. Regarded as one of the best architectural works of the twentieth century, the Pavilion embodies the main objectives that led to the institution of the Award: excellence and innovation in conceptual and constructional terms.
In 2009, Trade Fair Graz, Hall A is nominated by the Mies van der Rohe Award and it is highly recommended by the Jury.

Right: The space between its two layers accommodates the necessary escape stairs and lifts

Designer: Art & Build Architect **Location:** Strasbourg, France **Completion date:** 2008 **Photographer:** S. Brison, A. Zielonka

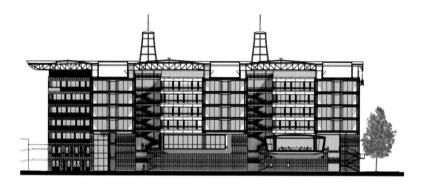

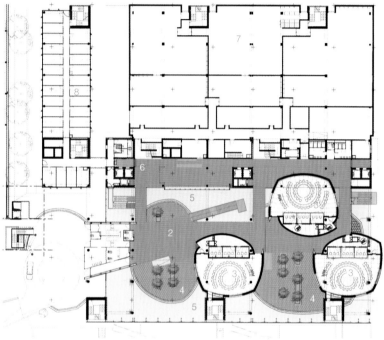

1. Entrance
2. Hall
3. Conference room
4. Lobby
5. Void on lobby
6. Corridor
7. Archives department
8. Offices

Right: General View

Agora Building – New General Building – Council of Europe

The new general building consists of offices, conference rooms, logistic centres, on-site social facilities (i.e. day-care centres/crèches) and car parks. By integrating the various functions in the one place, the architects have created a livable space, an ambiance which fosters the interaction of people and a belonging to the Council of Europe.

The forms of the buildings take their inspiration from the local countryside, sensitive to their specific geographical location and conveying a balance between their urban and pastoral settings.

A study of the building set-up was carried out, taking into account the temperate continental climate in a basin. At the centre of the building, the atria contribute to the connection between the office spaces and the many conference rooms. Its rooms with pre-patinated copper walls convey the solid foundations of the institution. The building has a mixed ventilation system: natural ventilation + double-flow ventilation. The broad textile chimneys play a role in the natural ventilation of the atria. Because the climate in Strasbourg is ultra continental, heat and humidity rise quickly.

The air that enters through the base of the glass façades is cooler because it comes in from the side that faces the canal. The solar chimneys that evacuate the hot air in the upper part of the building circulate the air in the atria naturally to create greater comfort for the occupants. In addition to the convivial appearance, the atria act as buffer zones between the outside and the office areas. The conference rooms have natural diffuse light that comes in through the envelope of the atrium.

Awarded:
2008 MIPIM Award / Business Centre Category
2008 BEX Award / Sustainable Development Category
2008 Nominee for LEAF Award / Best Sustainable Project
2009 Nominee for RICS Award / Best Sustainable Project
The MIPIM Awards recognise excellence and innovation in the real estate arena. The high-profile event attracts global attention from key industry players who come together to celebrate the winners in the following categories: Business centres, Green buildings, Hotel and tourism resorts, Refurbished office buildings, and Residential developments.
BEX brings together senior executives from across the value chain tasked with funding, delivering and operating major projects. This multi-disciplinary event is now in its sixth year and brings together leaders in property and construction

from both the public and private sector to exchange expertise and to do business together. The focus of the programme in the year of 2008 is on the funding and delivery of sustainable communities with particular emphasis on EU policy as the driving force behind investment in sustainability.

According to their philosophy of creating sustainable and environmentally-friendly designs, the Art & Build scheme integrates quality environmental targets. In particular, these are the choice of materials regarding the production, transportation, implementation, evolution and their ageing, and also the technical, ecological and economic choices made during the design, construction and life-span of the building.

Left: The atria contribute to the connection between the office spaces and the many conference rooms

Baiyun International Convention Centre

Designer: BURO II & Architecture Design Institue of CITIC South China (Group) **Location:** Guangzhou, China **Completion date:** 2007 **Photographer:** Philippe Van Gelooven

Located in the northern suburb of Guangzhou, the Baiyun Mountain was given the name "White-cloud" in Chinese because its main summit is often covered with clouds. Not only the natural landscape, but also the historical places on the mountain have made it the main attraction in Guangzhou throughout history.

The administration of the booming city of Guangzhou decided to develop a new administrative centre to the north of the downtown area, on the site of the old airport, at the edge of the historical landscape of the Baiyun Mountains. The new conference centre must function as the motor of this new urban process.

Here is the functional organisation of the building. The functional surfaces are logically grouped through a combination of horizontal and vertical functional modules. The horizontal modules are grouped in a two-storey base. They house the general services: the entrance halls, the main foyers, the general catering services (kitchens and restaurants), the multifunctional exhibition and banquet halls, a VIP area, the offices for management and supervision, the media centre and the main circulatory connections. The vertical modules consist of five blocks housing specialised activities. Each of these can function independently or be linked to the others (through the horizontal base).

The conference centre is housed within the three central blocks. The northern block includes an exclusive meeting hall and an auditorium that seats 2,500 people. The central block houses the middle-size halls, and the southern block the halls for 1,000 and for 500 people.

The hotels are located in the end-buildings, with 500 rooms in the northern building and 600 rooms in the southern block. They are linked to the conference centre at ground level and at roof level. They house restaurants and bars, dance halls, clubs, business centres, fitness centres, etc.

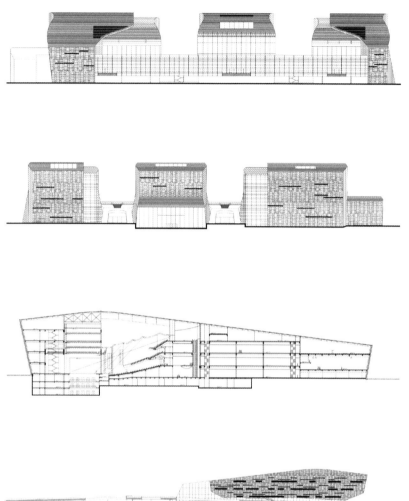

The façades are clad with local historical stone of feldspathic quartz sandstone with small window strips

Awarded:
World Architecture Festival Barcelona 2008
Winner in Civic Category

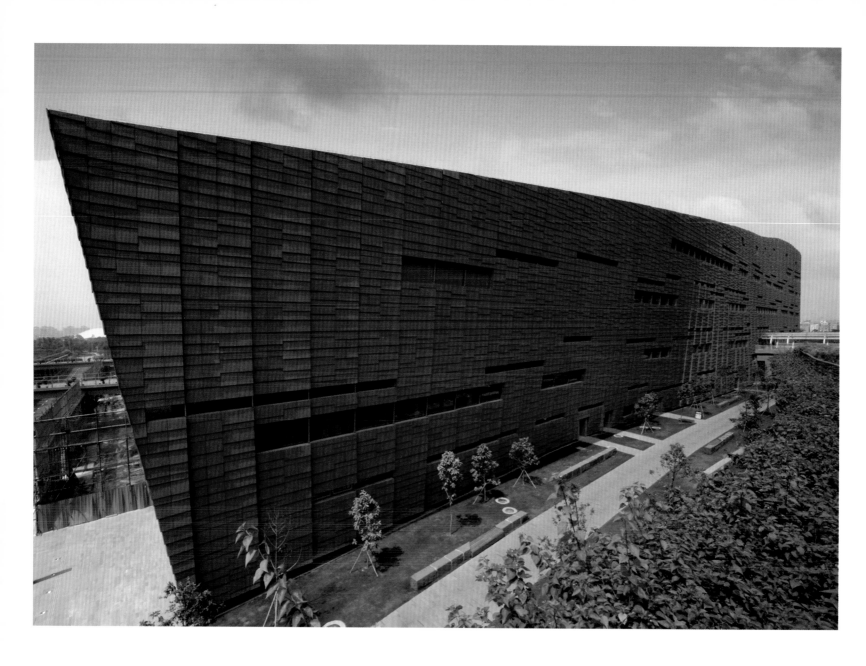

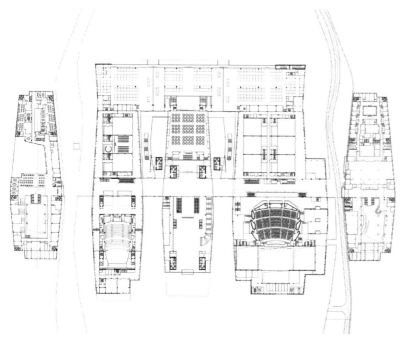

Top left: Entrance hall
Bottom left: Typical corridor

Kielder Observatory

Designer: Charles Barclay Architects **Location:** Northumberland, UK **Completion date:** 2008
Photographer: Charles Barclay Architects

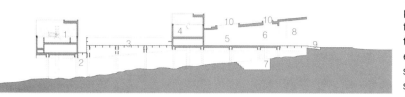

1. Pulsar turret
2. Galvanised steel escape stairs
3. Observation deck
4. Meade turret
5. Warm room
6. Entry hall
7. Compositing vault
8. Covered entrance area
9. Concrete ramp
10. Roof lights

The design brief called for an inexpensive building suitable to house two telescopes and a warm room, primarily intended for amateurs and outreach work but also suitable for scientific research. The design had to achieve a positive relation to the exposed setting on top of Black Fell overlooking Kielder Water and had to include both the facilities needed in this remote site and a "social space" for interaction and presentations, while being accessible both literally and culturally.

Timber was chosen as the material for the observatory early in the design process. Besides being a low-carbon material and the obvious relation to its forest setting, CBA wanted a low-tech engineering aesthetic for the observatory, the opposite of the NASA-inspired world of high tech, high expense and exclusive science. Instead, the designers wanted to evoke the curious, ad-hoc structures that have served as observatories down the ages, and the timber structures of the rural/industrial landscape at Kielder, the pit props of small coal mines and the timber trestle bridges of the railway that served them. They felt that a beautifully hand-crafted timber building with "Victorian" engineering would be more inspiring in this setting than seamless, glossy domes.

The observatory accommodation was arranged sequentially as a series of event spaces, creating a "promenade architecturale" and the possibility of having a number of separate groups on the observatory at the same time. The sequence starts with the covered entrance area with a bench seat and astronomer's notice board, and an opening that acts as the only window in the building. From here you enter the warm room, illuminated by rooflights, where slide lectures can be held or astronomers can conduct all-night vigils using computers to control the Meade telescope in the small turret next door. Double doors lead from the warm room to the gangway and then to the observation deck between the turrets. You descend a ramp to the entrance to the Pulsar turret where the elegant Pulsar 20 inch telescope is gradually revealed as you ascend a second, spiral ramp to the raised observation floor.

The very high wind loads combined with cantilevered elements called for higher strength timbers than the fast-growing Sitka Spruce that is grown at Kielder. Siberian larch was used for the secondary structure and cladding, American Douglas Fir for the timber columns and cantilever beams and European redwood for other framing elements. The spruce and birch plywood linings utilise stressed-skin technology to brace the cantilevers, and special non-slip decking ensures safety during icy conditions. The timber structure has transverse and longitudinal cross-bracing and the cast concrete approach ramp helps to anchor it to the hillside.

Awarded:
RIBA award 2009
Civic Trust Award 2009
Timber in Construction – Pride in Public Buildings Award 2008
Hadrian Award 2009

Top right: Exterior looking southwest
Bottom right: Exterior looking north

Top right: Entrance
Bottom right: Pulsar rotated

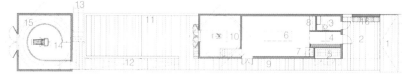

1. Entry ramp	9. Gangway
2. Covered entrance area	10. Meade turret
3. WC	11. Observation deck
4. Entrance	12. Ramp
5. Battery cupboard	13. Escape stairs
6. Warm room	14. Pulsar turret
7. Stove	15. Circular ramp
8. Kitchen	16. Bench seat

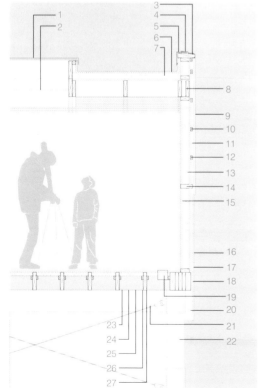

1. Rooflight
2. Exposed roof joist to warm room
3. Larch coping
4. Weather seal strip
5. Zinc trim
6. 20mm asphalt
7. 90mm rigid insulation
8. 250x50 softwood joists
9. 20mm vertical board on board larch cladding
10. 25x50 horizontal battens
11. Breather mernbrane
12. 18mm WBP spruce ply
13. 150mm quilt insulation
14. 125x50 softwood studs
15. 12mm WBP spruce ply
16. 20mm horizontal weatherboard larch cladding
17. 25mm clear air space
18. Continuous insect mesh
19. 300x140 floor vents
20. 150x50 skirting stanchion
21. 300x125 douglas fir cantilever beams
22. 250x250 douglas fir columns
23. 20mm softwood floorboards
24. 12mm ply subfloor
25. 50mm rigid insulation
26. 25x50 softwood battens
27. 250x50 softwood floor joists

Top left: Pulsar telescope
Bottom left: Meade telescope
Bottom right: Circular ramp

Mora River Aquarium

Designer: Promontorio Architects **Location:** Alentejo, Portugal **Completion date:** 2006 **Photographer:** Sérgio Guerra and Fernando Guerra

The River Aquarium is located in Mora, a small municipality in the Northern Alentejo region. Given the need to shift regional development from the dependence of an increasingly weaker agriculture economy into the environmental tourism and leisure market, the municipality launched a design-and-build competition for an aquarium that could somehow embody the paradigms of biodiversity of the Iberian river.

Integrated in the Ecological Wild Park of Gameiro and bordering the Raia stream, the building stands amidst a secluded field of cork and olive trees removed from the more intense leisure and fishing activities of the river. The plot's gently undulating topography forms a basin at the confluence of two small watercourses. Placing the aquarium at the edge of this quasi-natural retaining lake brought together the fundamental relation between its thematic contents and the presence of fresh water.

Given the blazing Alentejo sun and the need to create shade, the building was devised as a compact and monolithic volume with a pitched shelter of thin white pre-cast concrete porticos with single spans of 33 metres, evoking the profile of the canonical Alentejo whitewash barns known as "montes". The shading and cross ventilation systems along with the water circuits foster the reduction of cooling energy, the sustainable increase of humidity and the wellbeing of animal and plant life. Standing on a massive concrete plinth with a built-in stairway-cum-ramp entry, the pitched shed veils a set of mute boxes that contain the programme, namely reception, ticketing and shop, cafeteria, changing exhibits hall, documentation centre, research and education, live exhibits, multimedia and a small auditorium.

Inside, the exhibition spaces tend to be dark, in order to minimise UV impact on the live exhibits and allow visitors an in-depth viewing of the aquarium. The outdoor void between these programme boxes and the pitched shed generates not only accelerated viewpoints onto the outside, but also a promenade that culminates in the passage through a bridge over the lake which, in itself, is also a live exhibit of animals and plants collected and nurtured in the region.

Awarded:
VI BIAU Work Award
Award for Best Architectural Work in Ibero-America, built between 2004-2006, Second Prize
VI Bienal Ibero-americana de Arquitectura y Urbanismo, 2008

Right: Thin white pre-cast concrete porticos with single spans

Left: Lighting effect at night

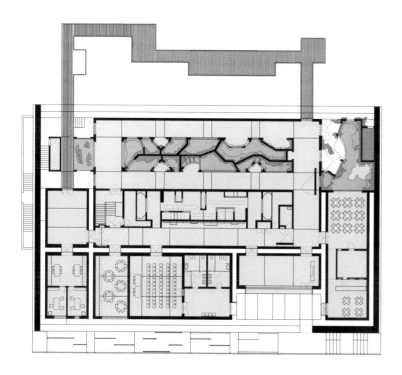

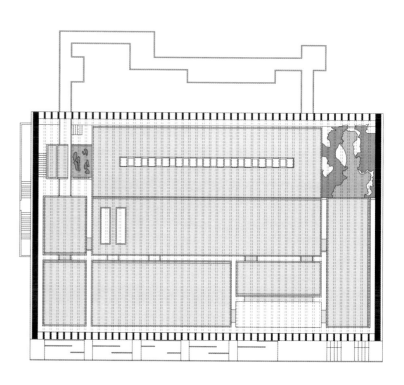

Left: Concrete colonnades in the sunlight create a four-dimensional space
Right: The inner view of the aquarium

Home.Haus – Home for Children and Adolescents

Designer: J. Mayer H. Architects & Sebastian Finckh **Location:** Hamburg, Germany **Completion date:** 2008 **Photographer:** Dirk Fellenberg

German architects J. Mayer H. and Sebastian Finckh have completed Home.Haus, a foster home for children and adolescents in Hamburg, Germany. The building is located next to a forest and has facilities for twelve girls and boys. The home includes a sports and music room. There is also a toddlers' room, kitchen and living room.

The home, which is located near the edge of the forest, has a two-colour relief façade which embraces the house's compact volume. There is a central staircase which penetrates the floors, creating an open space, encouraging communication amongst the youths who live there.

There are personal rooms and common rooms. In the study room the children can study knowledge. In the so-called independent group the children can try to have an independent life. In this home the interest and the talent of the children will be well developed. Except the normal rooms there are also a small baby room, a kitchen and a living room for everybody.

The building gets its external character with the relief and two-tone designed façade. Through the interwoven relief façade and the horizontal, ribbon-like structure on the sides, the windows are grouped together. On the gable ends the tapes go in a highly abstract tree motif, creating a special relationship to environment and use.

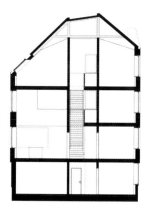
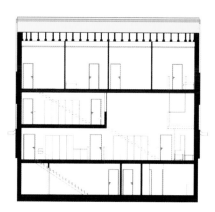

Right: Two-tone designed façade

Awarded:
BDA Hamburg Architecture Prize 2010, Third Prize

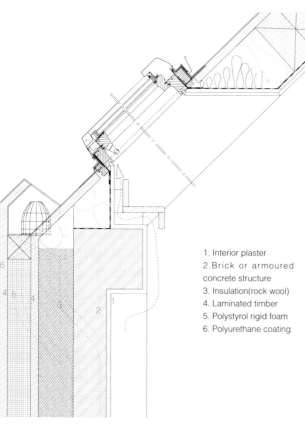

1. Interior plaster
2. Brick or armoured concrete structure
3. Insulation(rock wool)
4. Laminated timber
5. Polystyrol rigid foam
6. Polyurethane coating

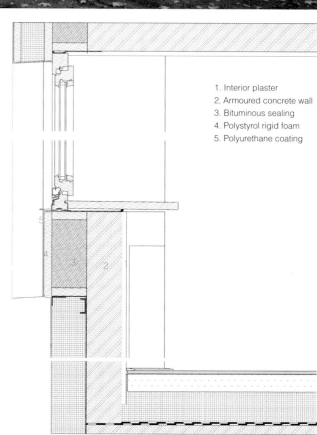

1. Interior plaster
2. Armoured concrete wall
3. Bituminous sealing
4. Polystyrol rigid foam
5. Polyurethane coating

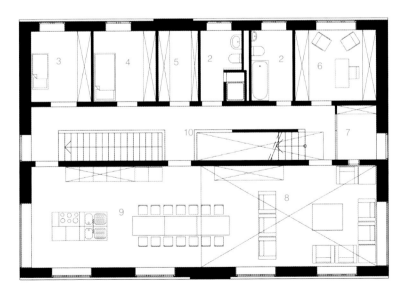

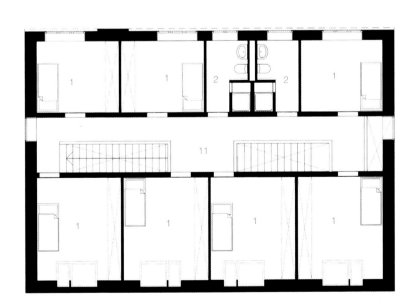

1. Rooms
2. Suite bathroom
3. Toddler rooms / infant room
4. Ready room / room attendance
5. Pantry / larder
6. Office
7. Porch / vestibule
8. Lounge / living zone
9. Cooking & dining / kitchen and dining zone
10. Stairway—staircase on ground floor
11. Stairwell / staircase attic floor

Left: Central staircase which penetrates the floors, creating an open space

Beth Sholom

Designer: Stanley Saitowitz | Natoma Architects **Location:** San Francisco, CA, USA **Completion date:** 2008 **Photographer:** Rien van Rijthoven, Bruce Damonte

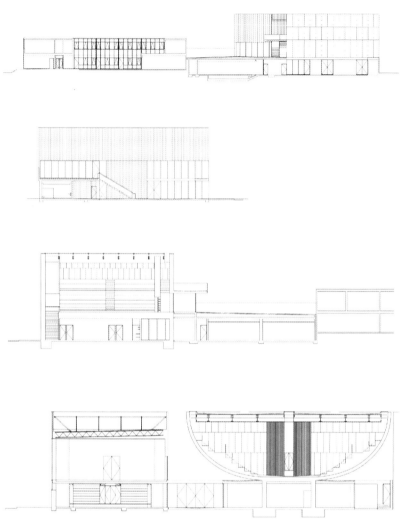

The design for the sanctuary begins from the inside with the creation of a sacred room, a space in the round, focussed on the centre from where the services are conducted. The format of two facing tiers of seating is the shape of the earliest synagogue remains at the fortress of Masada.

Jewish tradition equates iconography with idolatry – images are forbidden. The space is abstract, without figuration. One of the few symbols of Judaism is the seven branched candle, the menorah. Here a shadow menorah, changing as the sun moves through the day, animates the walls. All light enters the room from above, with views of the sky creating a sense of sanctity and removal in the midst of the noise and bustle of the city.

The first religious structure of the Jews was the tabernacle, described by Moses in Exodus, and carried in the wanderings through the desert. The text constantly focuses on the means of connection of the parts, rather than what is connected, as though the building itself is a metaphor for the community it joins.

Here the roof floats over the cup and is connected with light. The ceiling is sliced by the sky. By night it is lit with stars of light. The expression of this interior is the exterior of the building. The exterior also remembers the Western Wall in Jerusalem, using the colour and form of the stones of the ancient temple. From the lower entry court, the chapel is the first space. This is where daily morning and evening services are held. Like an old Beith Midrash (house of learning), the room is intimate with seating all around the walls. This is the repository of the history of the community, where the salvaged stained glass from the previous synagogue wraps the room. Across the court are the administrative offices, meditation space, library, and meeting rooms, which open onto a small garden below the bowl.

Awarded:

2009 AIA SF Design Awards / Honour Award, Excellence in Architecture
2008 46th Annual PCI Design Award / Best Institutional Building
2008 California Construction Awards / Best Religious Facilities
2008 World Architecture Festival / High Commendation Award, Religion & Contemplation
2008 Faith & Form Award / Honour Award, Religious Architecture – New Facilities
2008 Kirby Ward Fitzpatrick Award / Best Building in San Francisco
AIA San Francisco's Design Awards programme celebrates the best in architecture and urban design in the Bay Area. Recognising achievement in a broad range of architectural work by members and nonmembers, the programme serves to inform the public of the breadth and value of architectural practice.

The site is in San Francisco, in the flat Richmond district, at the intersection of Park Presidio and Clement Street. An early plan established a pair of religious structures as gateposts along this boulevard. One is the strong presence of the neo-classical Christian Science Church. The other is Congregation Beth Sholom, where an old synagogue was demolished to build this new building.

A plinth is established. Here all the non-religious programmes of the campus are contained. On the plinth two buildings are placed, forming a courtyard. One is a reflective cube, the social hall, the other a masonary structure, the

Right: The reflective cube is the social hall, and the masonry structure is the sanctuary

1. Entry courtyard
2. Reception / administration
3. Chapel
4. Library
5. Meditation room
6. Office
7. Meeting room
8. Kitchen
9. Garden courtyard
10. Restroom
11. Sanctuary
12. Plaza
13. Social hall
X. Existing

sanctuary, a vessel floating in air.

The origins of this structure are ancient. Solomon's Temple, built in Jerusalem after the Jews returned from exile in Egypt, was a procession of courts, ending with the Holy of Holies.

Here, the entry sequence establishes the distinction of a sacred place in the city through passage. It is a circular journey of turning and rising and turning. The first point of arrival is the lower court from which a staircase ascends to the courtyard. Here the three elements of the complex, sanctuary, social hall and existing school are connected. This circular route enables the sanctuary to be entered from the west facing the ark of torahs in the east, an important liturgical requirement.

Bottom left: On the plinth two buildings are placed, forming a courtyard

Top right: A slice of sky in the ceiling turns into the eternal light

Salvation Army Chelmsford

Designer: Hudson Architects **Location:** Chelmsford, UK **Completion date:** 2009 **Photographer:** Keith Collie

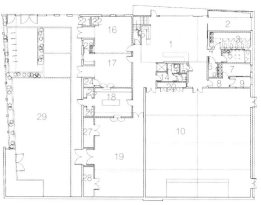

1. Foyer
2. Multi-purpose room
3. Female WC
4. Toilet lobby
5. Male WC
6. Disable WC
7. Centre manager
8. Lobby
9. Drop-in space/cry room
10. Worship hall
11. WC
12. Baby change
13. Cleaner
14. Lobby
15. Storage
16. Lounge
17. Hall 2
18. Kitchen
19. Hall 1
20. Storage
21. Bin storage
22. Storage
23. Baby WC
24. Storage
25. Cool storage
26. Dry storage
27. Storage 1
28. Storage 2
29. Courtyard
30. Commanding officer
31. Admin office
32. Instrument storage
33. Landing
34. Storage
35. Plant room
36. Plant roof
37. Void

The £2 million building provides 900 square metres of new accommodation for the mission on the site of its former premises. The new centre reflects the two sides of the mission, providing an assembly hall for worship as well as recreational facilities for the wide range of community outreach activities that The Salvation Army provides, such as an old people's day centre, youth activities and toddler care. The building's plan recognises that these two aspects are interconnected whilst offering flexibility and separation to permit activities to function simultaneously. An indoor sports hall, outdoor play area, lounge, kitchen and foyer with reception café facilities are arranged around a 310-seat worship hall, with administration offices located on the first floor.

The project pioneers modern methods of construction in its use of cross-laminated timber panel system KLH. The system is akin to jumbo plywood and offers all the advantages of reinforced concrete construction without the environmental cost. All walls and floor plates arrived on site as prefabricated panels with cut-outs for doors and windows, ready for quick assembly, allowing the building's frame to be erected in just 24 days. The two most conspicuous elements of the scheme which maximise the cross-laminated technology are the entrance canopy on the North elevation, which provides lateral stability to the front elevation, and the building's signature undulating butterfly roof, which rises to accommodate six generously sized dormer windows, measuring 4.2 m wide.

The butterfly roof is further dramatised by a zinc cladding, which cloaks the building and sweeps down and anchors it on its North elevation on Baddow Road and South elevation on Parkway. The zinc cloak forms a striking enclosure, which gives the building a very robust toughened and urbanistic character and distinguishes it from the surrounding brick buildings.

A 13 m tall x 3 m wide tower, made from the longest piece of KLH available, creates a contemporary steeple on Parkway, giving the building a strong street presence to passing traffic on the A138. The bronze steeple is clad in a radiant light film, which reflects a spectrum of colour, enshrining the cruciform symbol at its centre.

The building's toughened zinc shell breaks at the Baddow Road entrance lintel where floor-to-ceiling glazing creates a dialogue between the foyer café and the street, projecting an image of openness crucial to the work of the organisation. The east elevation on Goldlay Road and west elevation facing courtyard are both clad in brightly coloured rock panel board. On Goldlay Road the entire elevation has been CNC router pattern cut with a bespoke graphic indicative of the work of The Salvation Army.

Inside the 320-seat worship hall is the most dramatic space within the building, measuring 17m x 17m. It is in this room that Hudson Architects, working with Techniker Ltd KLH's specialist engineers, have exploited the plate-like organisation of the KLH system, pushing the spans of the roof and how it is supported. Unlike the foyer space, which is lined with mdf panels, in this room the raw KLH structural panels are treated with an intumescent varnish but left exposed so that walls and roof plate read as one sculptural form. The room is toplit by dormer windows on the east and west elevations and a square window on the Parkway elevation. Acoustic panels line the lower half of the walls to strengthen the hall's acoustics and minimise noise pollution to neighbouring residences. The room is hung with bespoke contemporary chandeliers manufactured by concord:marlin.

Right: The zinc cladding

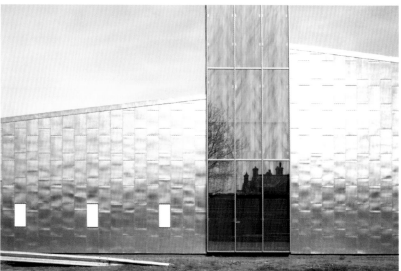

Awarded:
RIBA East Building of the Year 2009
RIBA East Community Award 2009
ACE/RIBA Award for Religious Architecture 2009

Top left: The entrance
Bottom left: View from the street
Top right: The courtyard

Left: The lounge
Right: Auditorium

Viikki Church

Designer: JKMM Architects **Location:** Helsinki, Finland **Completion date:** 2005 **Photographer:** Arno de la Chapelle, Jussi Tiainen, Kimmo Räisänen

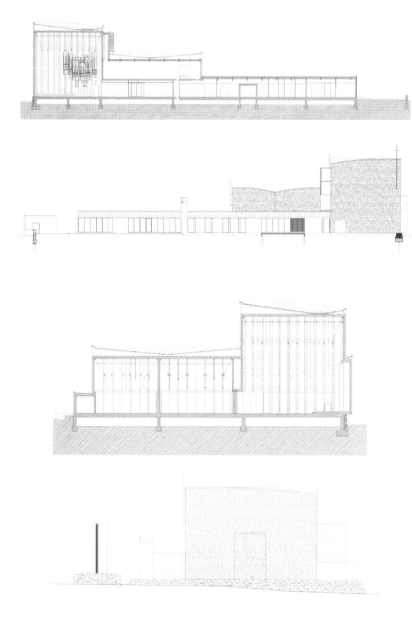

The church is located at the termination point of a narrowing landscape space, along the edge of a new square. The architecture evokes impressions of the Finnish forest. The eaves following the roof shapes reflect the forms of the treetops surrounding them. The approach to the church from the square takes a route past the bell tower and arrangements of vines. In the halls of the building the rising lines of the timber structures, resembling foliage, meet the systems of beams that define the space with light filtering through the structural members. The spaces, made of a single material, are hollowed out within the building like clearings in a forest.

The church design is based on the winning entry to an architectural competition for the Latokartano centre in Viikki, organised in 2000. The competition aimed to find suitable townscape and functional concepts for the civic and public service buildings of the area. The design brief also included proposals for the organisation of a public square, a park and commercial buildings on the competition site. In the chosen entry the public buildings form rectangular shapes that delineate the square and the park, their light-coloured brick surfaces differentiating them from the wooden church rising in their midst.

Already at the competition stage the contractee's wish was to execute a modern timber church on the site. During the design phase, the designers studied both traditional and new structural concepts. The building was designed with a view to achieving the architectonic goals reasonably and economically using prefabrication. The prefabricated components were joined seamlessly into one architectonic entity.

The materials used for the surfaces are durable and easy to repair and maintain during the course of time. The façades are clad with aspen, the surfaces of the congregation spaces lined with machine-split shingles, and the recreational rooms with horizontal boarding. Vertical slats were used for the bell tower. The untreated façades will gradually take on a grey patina. Radially sawn spruce has been used as a wall lining and flooring material in the congregation spaces. The objective of this solution was to minimise moisture movement of the timber, to achieve a uniform appearance, and to improve the durability of the floor. The spruce surfaces have been washed with lye. They were easy to clean during construction and to renovate in use. All building services were integrated into the ceiling construction and, the form-pressed, veneered panels also function as acoustic elements.

The commission included unique furnishing designs specifically for this interior. The double chairs for the church were designed to create the impression of long church pews. With their light colour, the aspen furnishings stand out well against the spruce surfaces. The texture of the split wood surfaces of the altar and the font highlights their important role. The altar triptych gives the chancel a serene atmosphere. Artist Antti Tanttu's work "Elämän Puu" (The Tree of Life) evokes impressions of an old mirror as light falls on its surface, changing the hues of the silver leaf surface. In the same way the church space, too, attempts to describe something that is beyond words.

Right: Shake-covered exterior

Awarded:

2006 Chicago Athenaeum's International Architecture Award

2007 Nominee for the Great Indoors Award

Chicago Athenaeum's International Architecture Award is the world's most prestigious global awards for new architecture, landscape architecture, interiors, and urban planning. The organisers of the Chicago Athenaeum include Museum of Architecture and Design, The European Centre for Architecture Art Design and Urban Studies, and Metropolitan Arts Press, Ltd.

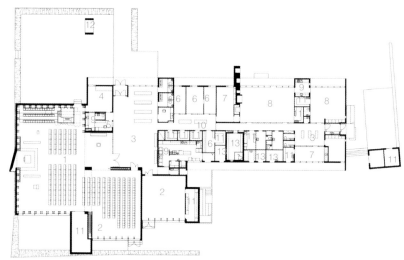

1. Church hall
2. Parish hall
3. Entrance hall
4. Sacristy
5. Hall porter
6. Office
7. Meeting room
8. Club room
9. Kitchen
10. Waiting room
11. Storage
12. Bell tower
13. Technical facilities

Left: Exterior view
Top right: Façade from south in the evening

Šiluva Pilgrim Information Centre

Designer: G.Natkevičius, E.Spūdys **Location:** Šiluva, Lithuania **Completion date:** 2009 **Photographer:** G.Česonis

1. Hall
2. Guest room
3. WC-shower
4. Cleaners room
5. Chapel
6. Restroom
7. Storage
8. Kitchen/dining room
9. Meeting room
10. Nuns room
11. Boiler room

Siluva is a provincial town in the centre of Lithuania with a population of 1,000 – one of the world's known pilgrim places, hosting the biggest religious feast in Lithuania every year in early September. The architect fostered the idea of redemption of the land between the Basilica and the Chapel from people, and installed a large square for worship, interconnecting the churches. Over the years, priests managed to buy surrounding lands, but the implementation of the architect's vision was prevented at the onset of the war. Only on the 400-year anniversary in 2008 did the state help to bring the idea to fruition.

Part of the central square is dedicated to mass rituals, facing the front of the Basilica and an outdoor altar in front of it. Its main plane is covered in milled cast concrete, like a pattern of Lithuanian fabric cut in rustic metal stripes. The light band of concrete is framed by a dotted line of black basalt blocks and green lawn. In order to preserve the fragile village scale, the designers narrowed the wide square space by framing it with rows of customised rustic metal chandeliers, seated trees, hedgerows, 3.5-m-high stone crosses/stations and solid oak benches. Thanks to these elements, the square is comfortable and functional both during mass events and on casual days when there are almost no one. Both the crowd and individual people are important elements of the square interior, creating its different moods.

In addition, the square area is broken by the two statues: a restored bronze St. Mary statuette and a bronze sculpture of Pope John Paul II who visited Siluva in 1993, created by Polish sculptor Ceslovas Dzvigajus for the quadricentennial anniversary.

At the edge of the square the designers designed the two-storey Siluva museum and its Pilgrim Information Centre. In order to avoid distortions of the square building scale, the building of the museum is divided into two gabled volumes, incorporated within the existing slope. The building is finished in two-colours and two-texture plaster, and the roof is covered with tin sheets of a very fine texture. The ground floor of the building hosts the aforementioned museum, information centre and public restrooms, and the upper hosts the hotel's guest rooms and living rooms, with the Siluva monks maintaining the complex. The two volumes' composition is strengthened by two integrated chapels within the design: one for guests, oriented to the Basilica, and one for monks, oriented to the Chapel.

Right: Side view of the house

Awarded:
2010 Best Realised Public Building

Left: The outside square
Top right: The façade of the house
Bottom right: The back side of the house

Left: Night view of the house

Right: The lobby and the stairs

AGSO Troonstraat

Designer: BURO II **Location:** Belgium **Completion date:** 2007 **Photographer:** Kris Vandamme

The "Troonstraat-Northlaan" project zone is one link in a series of large-scale sites between Troonstraat, Koningin Astridlaan and Nieuwpoortsesteenweg.

This chain of urban and regional activities that runs parallel to the sea dyke houses such activities as the Media Centre, the KVO football stadium, the Wellington race track, the Thermae Palace Hotel, the Royal Galleries, the KHBO campus, the town library and the municipal swimming pool. This multiplicity of functions was supplemented with a multifunctional basketball hall.

WIthin the architectural volume of the multifunctional sports hall, a separate "pit" is introduced to house the grandstand. This sculptural element runs around the entire basketball hall and is accentuated by wooden panelling underneath.

This venue will become the heart of all basketball activities. Underneath the tribune, the foyer is developed as a covered public space containing all the secondary functions of this multifunctional hall (cloakroom, ticketing, washrooms, store rooms, bar, etc.).

The grandstand seats 5,000 people (including 650 VIP seats). The VIP lounges are located at the top of the grandstand, ensuring good views of the playing court at all times. The other façades enjoy panoramic views of Northlaan and the Wellington race track.

1. Foyer
2. Media market
3. Changing rooms
4. Shopping
5. Open parking
6. The exit of the parking
7. The entry of the parking

Awarded:

2007 Belgian Building Awards

This is one of the most important architectural awards in Belgium. The project is a new link in the chain of urban and regional activities located between Troonstraat and Nieuwpoortsesteenweg, parallel to the boardwalk.

Right: The sculptural staircase

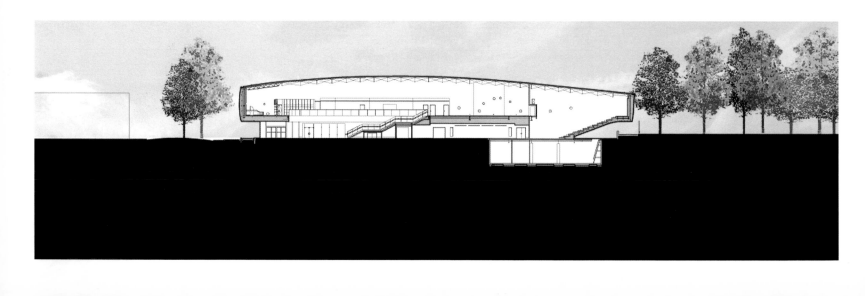

Bottom right: The wheelchair accessible in the venue

Gymnasium 46°09'N 16°50'E

Designer: STUDIO UP / Lea Pelivan & Toma Plejic **Location:** Koprivnica, Croatia **Completion date:** 2007 **Photographer:** Robert Les

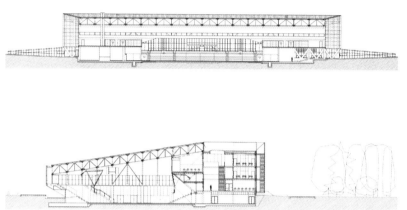

"Koprivnica – Spirit of Mega", a town with the lowest number of college graduates in Croatia announced the rebellious competition programme for 900 scholars and 2,000 spectators in 2003. The site of the high school building and a sports hall, in front of the American-like housing suburb periphery, is located at the end of a series of ambitious town interventions – mega elements.

The contact site of these "two worlds" is radically divided into two parts, black and green, full and empty, spiritual and physical, one facing the city and the other facing the residential suburbia.

The new building complex arises between these two extremes. An enigmatic compressed mono-volume of the gymnasium and sports hall complex with intricate spatial relations in contrast to a vast plain landscape, placed centrally on the plot, forms a gymnasium – a common place – a contrasting provocative whole lacking a foreground or background, without hierarchy or authority.

The selection of an abstract mono-volume, with a transparent membrane is a radical break with the modernist tradition of building schools and sports facilities as three-dimensional interpretations of bureaucratic disposition schemes.

The structure of the building is reinforced concrete on the ground floor, while the upper floors are realised with dry assembled H-shaped steel elements. The classrooms floors have thin slim-deck flooring, made up of trapezoid section lightweight galvanised sheet steel and cast concrete.

The roof of the sports hall uses a specially-designed grid work of right-angled elements and joints in steel. Generally, all the materials are available on the standard building market (lighting, anodised aluminium window frames, metal parapet grilles, Profilit industrial opal glass) and there is no finishing when unnecessary, as in case of the floor soffits which are left unfinished.

Because of its high cost, there is no air conditioning in the gym, so system of shutters above the sports hall and the ducts through the cantilevered classrooms of the top floor ensure a constant flow of cool air during the summer months, while the double polycarbonate skin creates a "green house effect" in winter. The translucent skin, illuminated at night, radiates the environment and turns the building into public condenser, an iconic and symbolic place for the youngsters of Koprivnica.

Awarded:

2009 Mies van der Rohe Awards – Emerging Architect Special Mention
The Award draws attention to the major contribution by European professionals to the development of new ideas and technologies. At the same time, it offers both individuals and public institutions an opportunity to reach a clearer understanding of the cultural role of architecture in the construction of our cities. Furthermore, the Award sets out to foster architecture in two significant ways: by stimulating greater circulation of professional architects throughout the entire European Union in response to transnational commissions and by supporting young architects as they set off on their careers.

Candidates for the Award are put forward by a broad group of independent experts from all over Europe, as well as from the architects' associations that form part of the European Council of Architects and other European national architects' associations. At each two-year edition, the jury selects two works:

Right: Entrance

one that receives the European Union Prize for Contemporary Architecture in recognition of its conceptual, technical and constructional qualities, and the other that receives the Emerging Architect Special Mention. The jury also selects a set of finalist works to be included in both the Award catalogue and exhibition.

For this project, the "common place" concept examines the stability of the hybrid, and enables the most diverse interpretations both in terms of use and interpretation of significance of the building.

In addition to the public-private partnership in construction of the gymnasium and sports hall in Koprivnica, the idea of building two complementary urban facilities in a single building also arose. Hybrid facilities overlap with the public-private partnership concept, where the hybrid complex is leased and managed independently of the newly-formed institution. The spatial and visual overlapping of the facilities and the synergy of use constitute the basic operative logic underlying the building.

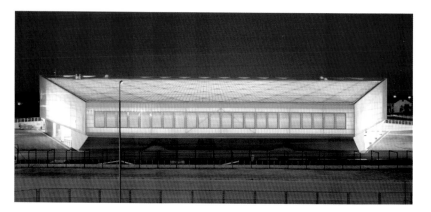

Top left: Position of the architecture in the context of the city Koprivnica
Bottom left: West polycarbonate façade
Top right: View of the sports hall from the telescopic stands
Bottom right: Bridges in the "street"

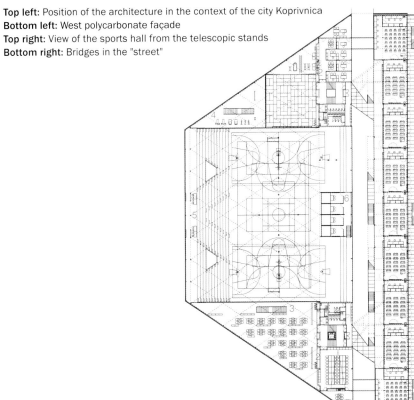

1. Classrooms
2. School administration
3. Lounge-restaurant
4. Gymnastics hall
5. Spectator stands
6. Direction

RELAXX

Designer: AK2 /Andrea Klimková & Peter Kruay **Location:** Bratislava, Czechoslovakia **Completion date:** 2008 **Photographer:** Ubo Stacho

The new building of sport and leasure centre RELAXX is situated on a long and narrow site in Einstein Street in Bratislava. It fits into a row of new mixed-use buidings between the Old and the New Bridge. Its nearest neighbours are furniture store Atrium, new office building of Tatrabanka and the Old Bridge. The site is surrounded by a busy traffic corridor of Highway ring from north and by an international railway track from south.

The basic shape of the building was determined by the long and narrow conditions of the site. The floorplan is approximately 100 metres long in its longest axis, 20 metres wide on western side and 14 metres wide on eastern side. Overall, the building can be described as both dynamic and poetic at the same time. Compact form is elevated on one side by two floors and sits on four up side-down U-shaped concrete pillars. The height of the lifted floor matches the height of the nearby Old Bridge. The other side of the building is set on a two-storey cuboid mass. With its overall six storeys, it is of the same height as the neighbouring furniture store Atrium.

The characteristic feature of this building is its play with transparency and opacity. Solid part of outer skin is covered by silver-grey titan-zinc cladding and wraps up the inner volume from top, back and bottom sides, creating a strong C-shaped profile figure visible from short elevations. North façade and two short side façades are transparent and fully glazed. Load-bearing structure is made of reinforced concrete monolith where the load-bearing system is based on columns and walls – all set up on basic 7.5x7.5 metres grid.

The main entrance into the building is provided by a pedestrian ramp and staircase from Einsteinova Street. In terms of function, the building is divided as follows: on the first floor there are retail and refreshment shops; the second floor is health and wellness centre; on the third floor there is indoor golf court, bio-restaurant, solarium and children's playground; the fourth and fifth floor is dedicated to sport and leisure activities divided into wet and dry zone. Dry zone on the fourth floor contains fitness, aerobics, yoga, spinning, changing rooms, whereas the wet zone on the fifth floor consists of swimming pool, whirlpool, sauna, massage room and snack bar.

Two underground storeys with parking and service rooms are accessible by ramps from both sides of the building. One of the ramps leads through an aisle between the U-shaped load-bearing pillars from east side of the building.

Awarded:

2008 Public Building on Einsteinova Street in Bratislava, Slovakia/First Prize in the Competition

A private investor invited selected architectural studios for a competition, the solution of a polyfunctional building on Einsteinova Street, Bratislava. The aim of the competition was to make the best account of the location for public facilities. The investor selected the proposal which gave the most satisfaction of his ideas. The design has enough of inventions and verifies criteria for efficiency of utilisation of plot.

During the projecting, this polyfunctional/public building was forming the functional use of it – sport and relaxing centre, a pool, wellness, fitness, indoor golf court integrated with cafés and fast-food restaurants. The project was completed in the year 2007, and the construction was completed in autumn 2008. The name of the building is RELAXX Sport and Leisure Centre in Bratislava.

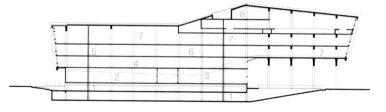

1. Garage
2. Coffee house
3. Fast food
4. Health care centre
5. Gastronomy
6. Shops
7. Sport facilities
8. Office wellness facilities – wet zone

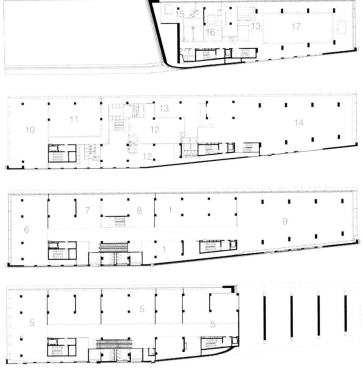

1. Shop
2. Coffee house
3. Entrance
4. Fast food
5. Health care
6. Bio-restaurant
7. Baby room
8. Reception
9. Indoor golf court
10. Aerobics
11. Spinning
12. Dressing
13. Bar
14. Fitness
15. Whirlpool
16. Sauna
17. Pool

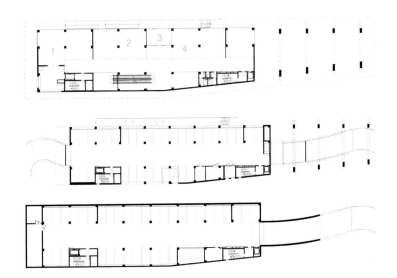

The Ring Football Stadium

Designer: OFIS arhitekti & Multiplan arhitekti **Location:** Maribor, Slovenia **Completion date:** 2008
Photographer: OFIS arhitekti & Multiplan arhitekti

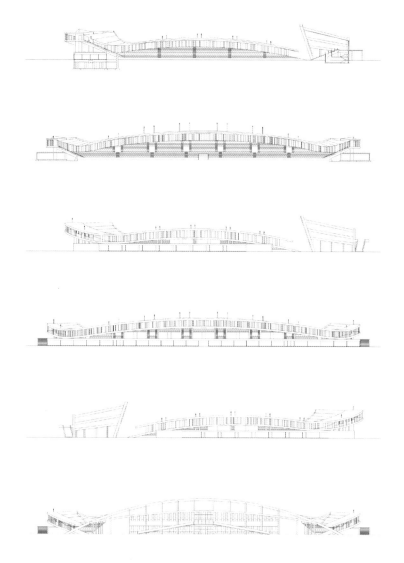

The brief was to convert the field into a football stadium and extend the existing building with covered tribunes (12,500 spectators, VIP and press facilities) and additional public programmes such as four big gymnasiums, fitness club with swimming pools, shops and restaurants. The project proposed a ring of tribunes woven above enclosed base with public programmes. The lowest and the highest point of the tribunes are defined by the quality of the view of the spectator.

In the corners of the field, where the views are restricted, the entrances to the tribunes are displaced. The ring is pulled down here to the level of the entry plateau. Then it rises gently and it reaches the highest point in the middle of the field. There the maximum number of the seats is provided, offering the best views to the field. The corridor of the ring has double skin and provids rooms for VIP, press and refreshments.

In the base, sport halls and shops are displaced. The roof of the base forms an entry plateau to the tribunes and also offers views to the smaller sport field at the side of the stadium.

In the past decade we have witnessed an unprecedented boom in the construction of sports stadiums. Most of the time, state-of-the-art technology, innovative structural engineering and enormous construction budgets have earned the stadiums the status of the new Cathedrals of the 21st century. The new football stadium in Slovene second biggest city Maribor might not be of an Olympic size; however, its exquisite architectural expression can join in the game of acquiring all of the prestigious adjectives.

The competition brief called for an addition to the existing 60s concrete shell, adding extra 12,000 seats and additional public programmes of four big gymnasiums, fitness club with swimming pools, shops and restaurants. OFIS' proposal clearly divided two functional elements, that of public programme and that of tribunes for spectators into two distinct forms. Public sports facilities are neatly packed on three floors bellow ground where its rectangular "roof" serves as a plateau for tribunes above. As a contrast to rectangular base, the main architectural feature of the project is the gently undulating ring, which embraces the tribunes around the perimeter. The ring serves as a hall and offers rooms for additional programme. Simultaneously it is a structural carrier of a translucent roof that elegantly hovers over the seating area inside the stadium.

The logic behind the setting of the undulation of the ring follows the idea of offering the best viewing positions to the visitors. Where the visibility of the football pitch is the lowest, the ring comes down and touches the plateau and where the visibility is the best, the ring reaches the highest point. "Blank" spots with low visibility are in return used as entry points to the tribunes. Clearly, what puts the design of the Stadium in Maribor on the map of world's stadiums is its conceptual precision. The orchestration of shapes with the existing concrete shell, its apparent simplicity of curved form and the selection of basic construction materials, all play part in generating an outstanding landmark building.

Right: Matte perspex on steel structure

Awarded:
2009 Mies van der Rohe Awards Nomination
1998 Competition First Prize
The Award draws attention to the major contribution by European professionals
to the development of new ideas and technologies. At the same time, it offers
both individuals and public institutions an opportunity to reach a clearer
understanding of the cultural role of architecture in the construction of our
cities. Furthermore, the Award sets out to foster architecture in two significant
ways: by stimulating greater circulation of professional architects throughout
the entire European Union in response to transnational commissions and by
supporting young architects as they set off on their careers.
The title RING was the entry code of the winning competition back in 1998.

Top right: The orchestration of shapes with the existing concrete shell

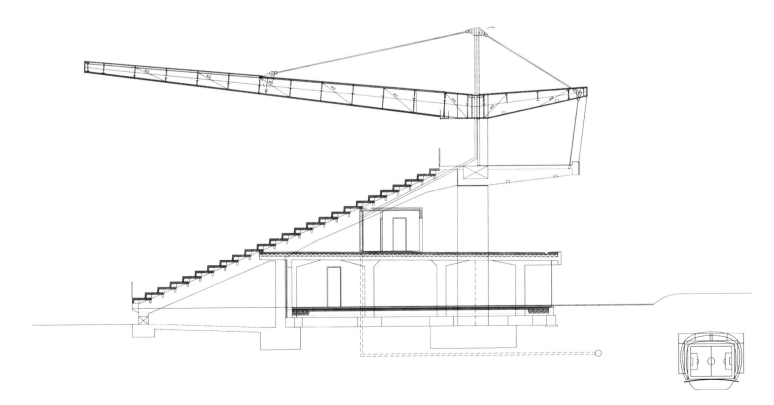

Left: The translucent roof elegantly hovers over the seating area inside the stadium

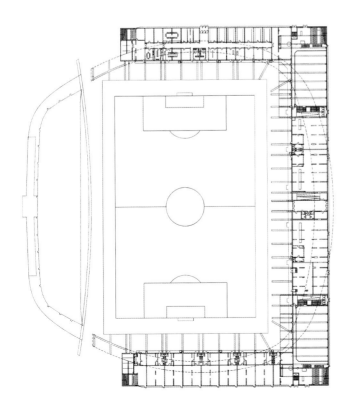

Century Lotus Sports Park

Designer: Volkwin Marg / gmp Architekten – von Gerkan, Marg and Partners Architects **Location:** Foshan, China **Completion date:** 2006 **Photographer:** Christian Gahl, Berlin

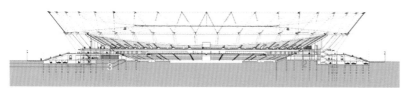

1. Auditorium
2. VIP / sponsoring area
3. Athletes / media / organisation

On the occasion of the 12th Guangdong Province Sports Meeting 2006, Foshan wanted to present itself to the public as a modern and growing city. A multipurpose stadium and a swimming hall serve all demands of international sports competitions, while training and leisure sports facilities offer a large variety of activities to the visitors.

The circular stadium dominates the silhouette of the sports park with its huge, white membrane roof. BEING Situated on a green hill, it looks like a lotus in blossom.

The stadium's spokes-wheel roof construction with the folded membrane covering measures 350 metres in diametre and covers not just the stands but the outer concourses as well. Above the field, the roof can be opened and closed according to demand. With a grand and generous gesture, it links the stadium bowl to the surrounding park and becomes a symbol for the games of 2006.

The second venue in the sports park, the swimming pool, reflects the architectural language of the stadium, allowing the two buildings to appear as an ensemble without undermining the unquestioned dominance of the stadium.

The translucent membrane roof appears to hover unsupported above the water, and the stands and pools are embedded into the plateau of dike topography. The pools are constructed in a series and set into ground which has been built up to a height of one or two storeys.

Unlike the stadium, the folding membrane over the swimming complex is held up by a linear structure of more than seventy-metres-long diagonal steel supports, whose tension is taken up by triangular abutments. Supporting cables stretch between these abutments ensuring the stability of the membrane roof.

The architectural practice von Gerkan, Marg and Partners was founded by Meinhard von Gerkan and Volkwin Marg in 1965. Since its inception it has grown to include four partners one partner for China eleven associate partners more then 500 employees in ten offices in Germany and abroad. gmp is one of the few practices with a generalist position, which takes responsibility for a project from the design idea and its realisation right through to the interior design.

Awarded:

2009 IOC/IAKS Award / Silver Medal

The IOC/IAKS Award is the only international architecture competition for sports and leisure facilities. Its aim is to bring to public attention exemplary buildings and complexes in which good functionality harmonises well with high-quality architectural design inside and outside, with environmental compatibility and with considerate integration into the urban or rural landscape.

Right: White membrane roof

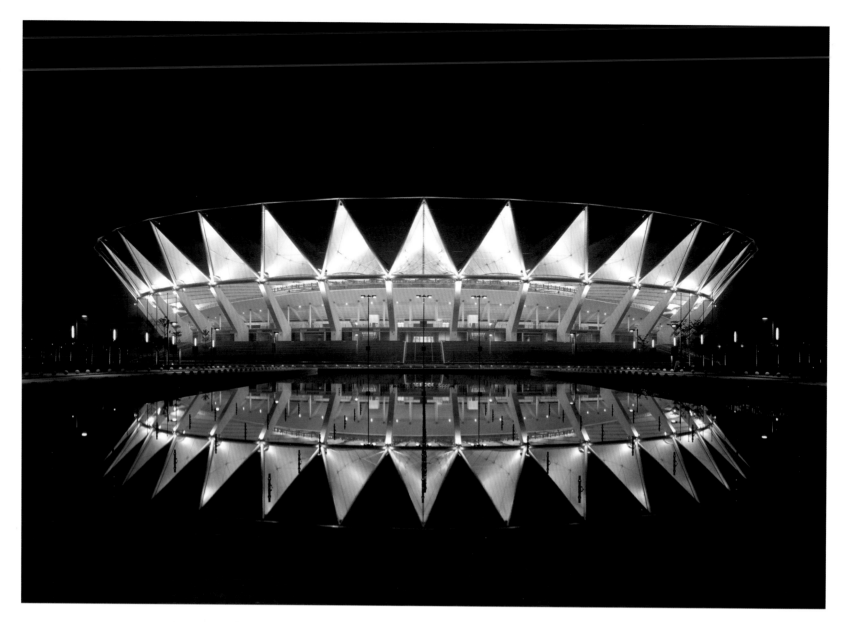

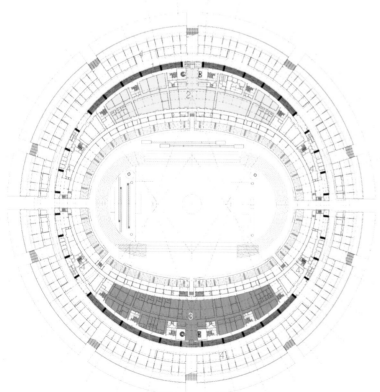

1. Auditorium
2. VIP / sponsoring area
3. Athletes / media / organisation
4. General surfaces

Left: Lighting effect of the stadium at night
Top right: Folded membrane covering measures 350 m in diameter

Top right: The translucent membrane roof appears to hover unsupported above the water

Sports Facilities, Universidad de los Andes

Designers: MGP Arquitecturay Urbanismo / Felipe González-Pacheco Mejía, Álvaro Bohórquez Rivero
Location: Bogotá, Colombia **Completion date:** 2009 **Photographer:** Andrés Valbuena

This project was awarded first prize in an architectural contest. The aim of the contest was to design a building for inner sports activities, which could blend with its outdoor surroundings. The site given for such challenge is called La Gata Golosa, located at the highest part of the University, in the boundaries between the city and the mountain in Bogotá, in a site of wonderful natural conditions, next to the emblematic Cerros de Monserratey Guadalupe. The city regulations were very strict in terms of site occupation, allowing the project to occupy the 5% of the whole lot. This implied proposing a compact building, locating the sport activities one on top of the other, in particular the pool and the multifunctional covered courts.

The result is a building decomposed in six architectural pieces set together in a way that the mountains, the city and the sky are involved in the project as part of the limits of the space. The strategy allows that each activity is seen by others, in a transparent building designed to prastice sports but also to see the practising of sports, encouraging the students to get involved with what it offers.

The limits of the spaces inside or outside are undefined, and the building offers an unlimited number of possibilities to move around from one activity to another. The high level of transparency of the architectural pieces lets the light and the sight go through the volumes, allowing the building to be scanned from any angle or level the observer is at.

From the technical point of view, the architectural design resolves the challenging but strong position of locating the pool in the upper level, above the main court, by making four concrete elephant feet attached by a metal structure, in a high-risk earthquake zone. In this way the floating pool could take advantage of the imposing presence of the mountains and the impressive city view.

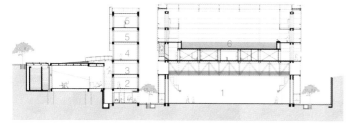

1. Multiple court
2. Cafeteria
3. Dance room
4. Student's room
5. Gym
6. Pool

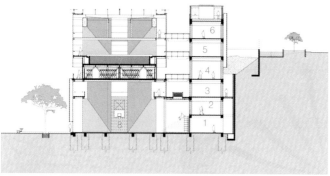

1. Storage/multipurpose court
2. Ping pong room
3. Board games room
4. Multipurpose room
5. Gym
6. Administration office
7. Pool
8. Multiple court

Awarded:
CEMEX Prizes, Colombia, May 2010
Institutional / Industrial Architecture – First Place
CEMEX International Prizes, October 2010
Institutional / Industrial Architecture – First Place

Right: Transparency of façade elements

Left: View from exterior court
Top right: Building's transparency
Bottom right: Between architectural pieces

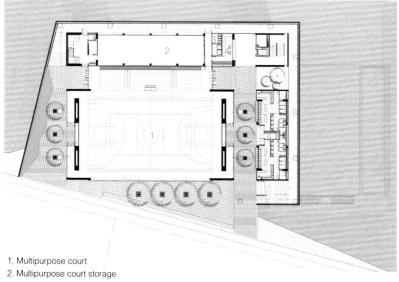

1. Multipurpose court
2. Multipurpose court storage
3. Security
4. Reception area
5. Changing room

Top left: Main access
Top right: Transparency between pieces
Bottom right: Practising sports and watching practising sports

Broad Institute

Designer: Elkus Manfredi Architects **Location:** Massachusetts, US **Completion date:** January 2006
Photographer: Anton Grassl / Esto

At the roof, the building terminates with a volumetric composition of voids and foils that form a rational and sculptural composition while integrating the 1.26-metre-tall mechanical penthouse needed to support laboratory systems.

Furthering the Institute's mission of community participation, the ground floor lobby functions as an interactive museum exploring the scientific, political, and social aspects of the research performed in the labs above.

The second floor contains flexible meeting rooms and a garden terrace that covers the loading dock, providing gathering and breakout spaces for up to 100 visitors and a direct link to the adjacent parking garage.

The laboratories on the western half of each floor consist of innovative BL1 and BL2 spaces with flexible bench cabinetwork, prep rooms, instrument rooms, and bioinformatics computation rooms. At the eastern half, office areas are organised around "science living rooms" and feature full-height glass partitions, encouraging staff interaction and facilitating daylight penetration.

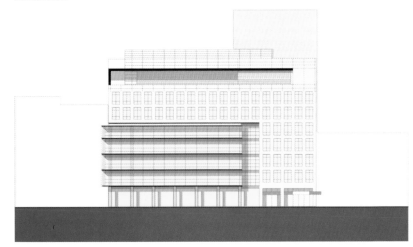

1. Loading
2. Lecture hall
3. Lobby
4. Parking
5. MBTA
6. Lab
7. Mechanical

Awarded:

2007 R&D Magazine, Laboratory of the Year, High Honour
The building's gridded façade creates a defined streetwall for the intersecting main street, while the prominent glass box that punctures the grid celebrates the terminus of the axis that comes diagonally to the site. Functionally, this glass box exhibits research activity to the street below while suffusing labs with natural light and a sense of openness.

Left: The building's gridded façade creates a defined streetwall for the intersecting main street
Right: The ground floor lobby is wrapped in full height glass and controls for digital information screens

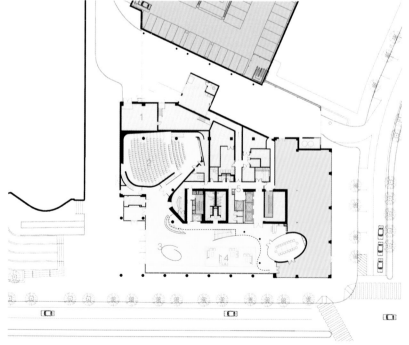

1. Loading
2. Lecture hall
3. Lobby
4. Lounge
5. Corridor

Left: Flexible meeting rooms provide gathering spaces for up to 100 visitors

Perimeter Institute for Research in Theoretical Physics

Designer: Saucier + Perrotte Architectes / André Perrotte **Location:** Waterloo, Ontario, Canada
Completion date: 2004 **Photographer:** Marc Cramer

Riding the controversial line between public and private space, this research institute attempts to subvert the usual hard thresholds established by private enterprise in the public realm. The site is on the shore of Silver Lake, at the northern edge of Waterloo's downtown core and the southern edge of the city's central park. Adjacent to the primary pedestrian access between the university campus and the city centre, the site is an urban wilderness between clearly defined worlds.

The design takes inspiration from the wide-ranging, hard-to-define concepts that make up the subject matter of theoretical physics, at once micro- and macro-cosmic, rich in information and of indeterminate form and substance. Between the city and park, the Perimeter Institute expands and inhabits the improbable space of the line separating the two. The building defines the secure zones of the Institute's facilities within a series of parallel glass walls, embedded in an erupting ground plane that reveals a large reflecting pool. The north façade, facing the park across this pool, reveals the Institute as an organism, a microcosm of discrete elements. The south façade, facing the city across train tracks and the city's main arterial road, presents the Institute as a unified but transforming entity, of enigmatic scale and content. Entry to the Institute is possible from both the north, along the reflecting pool, and the south, under the new ground plane.

The interior of the Institute is organised around two central spaces, the main hall on the ground floor and the garden on the first. Spaces for administration, meeting and seminar rooms, leisure and fitness spaces, and a multipurpose theatre for symposia and public presentations, have direct access to the main hall. The circulation corridors running east-west are positioned between the opalescent glass planes, which are occasionally punctured and shifted to reveal views across the interior space of the hall. Vertical circulation climbs these walls, tendrils of ground that run from the garden through the building. The garden – nature emerging from the vacuum – is crossed by three bridges that puncture all the planes, as well as the north and south façades. The bridges provide quick access to information, facilities and research colleagues. These conduits, which formally bind together the Institute, are routes crossing the improbable space between theoretical physics and everyday life.

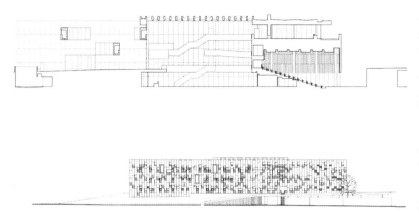

Right: South façade and erupting ground plane

Awarded:

2006 Governor General's Academic Medal

Lord Dufferin, Canada's third Governor General after Confederation, created the Academic Medals in 1873 to encourage academic excellence across the nation. Over the years, they have become the most prestigious awards that students in Canadian schools can receive.

For more than 125 years, the Governor General's Academic Medals have recognised the outstanding scholastic achievements of students in Canada. They are awarded to the student graduating with the highest average from a high school, as well as from approved college or university programmes. Pierre Trudeau, Tommy Douglas, Kim Campbell, Robert Bourassa, Robert Stanfield and Gabrielle Roy are just some of the more than 50,000 people who have received the Governor General's Academic Medal as the start of a life of accomplishment.

Today, the Governor General's Academic Medals are awarded at four distinct levels: Bronze at the secondary school level; Collegiate Bronze at the post-secondary, diploma level; Silver at the undergraduate level; and Gold at the graduate level. Medals are presented on behalf of the Governor General by participating educational institutions, along with personalised certificates signed by the Governor General. There is no monetary award associated with the Medal.

Top right: Northern entrance and reflecting pool
Bottom right: Northern façade, reflecting pool and auditorium

Left: Auditorium
Right: Cafeteria / space for informal group gathering and discussion

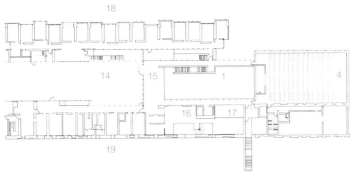

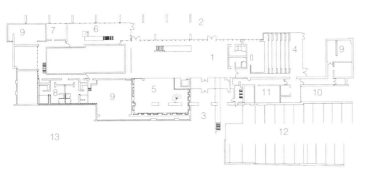

1. Main hall
2. North entrance
3. South entrance
4. Lecture theatre
5. Library
6. Lounge
7. Gym
8. Changing rooms
9. Mechanical
10. Loading dock
11. Storage
12. Parking
13. Squash (basement)
14. Garden
15. Mezzanine (hall)
16. Mezzanine of the library
17. Reading room
18. Researcher's offices
19. Administrative offices

Merck Research Laboratories Boston

Designer: KlingStubbins **Location:** Boston, USA **Completion date:** 2004 **Photographer:** Paul Warchol Photography, ChristopherBarnes.com

Merck Research Laboratories Boston is a 12-storey research laboratory tower with six levels of below-grade parking located in the Longwood Medical Area of Boston, a highly active educational, cultural, and historical environment. The site is at the juncture of high-rise institutional buildings to the west and south, and lower-scaled academic buildings to the east and north. As a result of the building's adjacencies, considerations of scale, material, function, and site geometry were paramount in the design process. The context within which MRL Boston exists is one toward which a sympathetic, not similar, response seemed appropriate. To achieve a singular identity, the materials and colouration chosen allow the building to present itself uniquely.

Massing is a direct reaction to the site limitations, and the very different context on each of the four sides. The laboratory tower is similar in scale to the research and health care facilities to the south, and the northern extension corresponds to the scale of Emmanuel College. The juncture between the two components is given definition by an atrium that is at the terminus of the entry drive. Here, the various geometries of the site converge to define the atrium space – a space that serves as a collector of people and events on the ground floor and as an artery that binds the tower to its lower wing with bridges on the second, third, and fourth floors.

The programme's resolution was the obvious point of departure; and although there existed many dictates respective to adjacency and interrelationship, the design was further influenced by concerns for flexibility and adaptability. The complex programme consists of chemistry, biology, and pharmacology laboratories, as well as offices, conferencing and interaction areas, cafeteria, auditorium, and library. The private functions of research are housed within the tower with restrictions of access. The open and shared spaces are located in the low wing with fewer access restrictions. Plan determinations were made with consideration for movement from public to private, and along routes which are conducive to promoting interaction.

The character of the building was influenced by issues of programme and adjacencies, but more directly by willful decisions involving imagery. The design is very much about the interface with light; no other consideration is seen as so contributory to ultimately providing a range of experiences. The building's enclosure, while satisfying criteria of comfort, containment, and security, is more about the myriad of presentation possibilities than it is about boundary. The architectural character endeavors to be understood in terms which are readily associated with scientific research, technology, discovery, and affording both the viewers of the building and the participants within layers of experience.

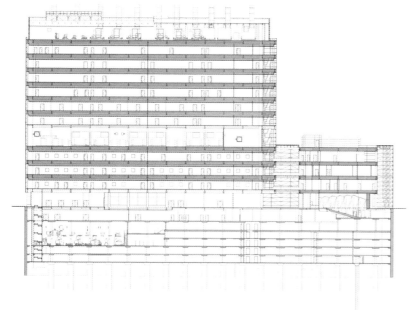

Right: View of entrance

Awarded:

2006 Building Information Model (BIM) Awards

The Building Information Model (BIM) Awards, given by AIA Technology in the Architectural Practice Knowledge Community (TAP), honour projects that highlight proven strategies and the latest trends in design and technology in the building industry.

2004, Gold Medal, AIA Philadelphia Chapter

"Doing a large building well is more difficult than doing a good small building. They have taken what is usually a very introverted programme and opened it into a beautifully layered structure. It has a sophisticated glass skin that allows lightness and special qualities to be revealed. It is beautiful, elegant and sophisticated. The different degrees of transparency allow spatial expression of interior volumes... literal and figurative transparencies. Compositionally, the scale of the building is a well-articulated series of volumes. The plans, sections and elevations of the building elegantly reduce from the urban scale to that of the user." Richard Gluckman, FAIA, speaking for the AIA Philadelphia Jury

Right: View of entrance from south

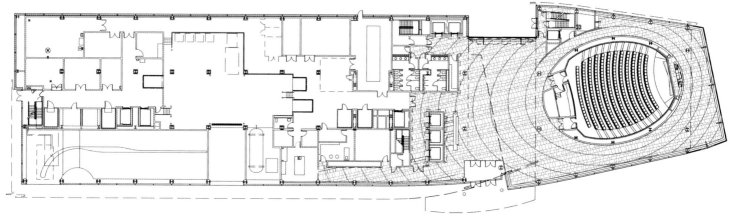

Left: View towards skylight indicating atrium curtain wall and canopy structure
View of staircase in north atrium
Right: Corridor from lobby leading to display laboratory

Top left: Reception desk
Bottom left: Auditorium
Top right: Typical chemistry lab
Bottom right: Corridor around auditorium

Highfields Automotive and Engineering Training Centre

Designer: Hawkins\Brown **Location:** Nottingham, UK **Completion date:** 2008 **Photographer:** Tim Crocker

The 6,600 sq m Training Centre brings into partnership Castle College, the largest provider of further education and community learning in Nottingham, and car manufacturer Toyota. Seen as an exemplar of collaboration, it provides high-level training and research facilities for automotive engineering, including hybrid engine technology and biofuels. Within the centre teaching staff and trained Toyota engineers work along side students and school children, making it the first centre in Europe to offer specialist training for 14 yrs through to adult in one location.

Located within the Highfields Science Park site, the building form continues the logic of the master plan, engaging with the central public space by allowing the landscape to flow through and around its structure. The imaginative form of the building is derived from the linear footprints of the other buildings on the master plan so that the building emerges like a new species from the same family of insects. It perches on the edge of a water meadow, accessed by the Science Park's central pedestrian spine "the lilypad boardwalk".

The two wings occupied by Castle College and Toyota extend out across the landscape, sheltering and screening 80 car parking spaces beneath. The wings feature the centre's principal facilities – ten 250-square-metre workshops, 1,100 square-metres of training and office space, breakout spaces and changing rooms. The wings are linked by a three-storey high hub, which contains all the communal spaces including a library and IT centre, restaurant and reception.

Clad predominantly in a glazed curtain wall, the hub is shaded by 160 capsule-shaped perforated panels held in place by a facetted cone around the building. The large volumes of the workshops are clad in finely ribbed silver composite panels and are supported by rows of smooth, circular concrete columns. The smaller training blocks are clad in a riot of mixed greens, nestling around and softening the bulk of the principal workshops.

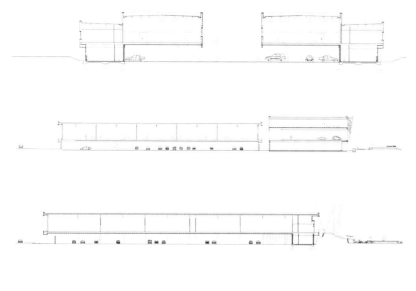

Awarded:
RIBA Award 2009
RIBA LSC Further Education Design Excellence Award 2009

Bottom right: The buildings are arranged around a central reed bed punctuated by timber lilypad-shaped decks

1. Entrance
2. Training room
3. Office
4. Workshop
5. Bodyshop
6. Storage
7. Mixing room
8. Engineering
9. MOT diagnostic and test
10. Lexus showroom
11. Toyota showroom
12. Vehicle access
13. Ramp and stairs to landscape
designer's specifications
14. Balcony

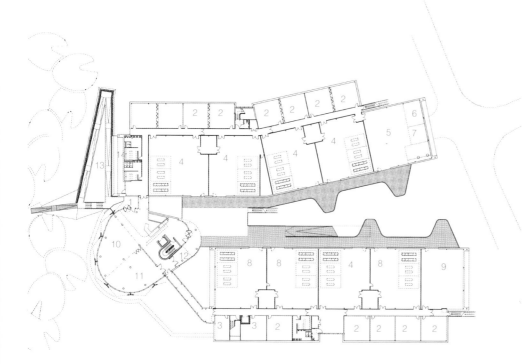

Left: The Hub is a learning and event space that is wrapped in "tyre-tread" solar shading,
composed of 160 capsule-shaped perforated panels

Samundra Institute of Maritime Studies

Designer: Christopher Charles Benninger Architects Pvt. Ltd **Location:** Pune, India **Completion date:** 2007 **Photographer:** A. Ramprasad

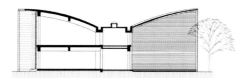

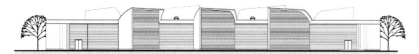

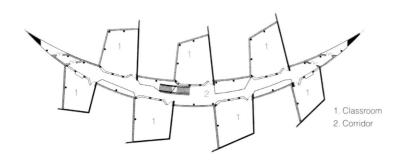

1. Classroom
2. Corridor

The Samundra Institute of Maritime Studies (SIMS) near Mumbai was established by Executive Ship Management (ESM) Singapore, to fulfill its new vision of an industry driven by environmental protection, safety and efficiency. Realising that it must drive this mission through human resources, it embarked on the creation of a sophisticated, state-of-the-art, world-class green campus where the full range of pre-sea and post-sea studies can be imparted.

Like ships floating upon a vast undulating sea, the sculpturesque buildings appear to float on the grass lawns. Steel and glass were employed to give the cadets a taste of sea life.

On the campus, which was completed in 2007, housing 480 cadets, energy efficiency begins to walk the talk with the campus producing 90 KW of energy through its photovoltaic panels, which lend unique character to façades whose appearance is driven by efficiency and not fashions! Photovoltaic cells, both translucent and opaque, became modern-day Indian "jaalis", allowing in natural light while blocking heat via the 300-foot-long photovoltaic solar wall in the Maritime Workshop; Asia's longest, it produces 90 KW daily! Operable glass on the north façade brings in natural light, giving the testing equipment and machinery all-round illumination and ventilation. The Administration Building cleverly exploits northern light through its wavy glass atrium wall, while generating electricity through the grand photovoltaic south-facing façade that produces 30 KW. The structure is made of two walls, like a ship, that fall apart in the middle and then rejoin back in the end.

The long Students Hostel structure, which is 250 metres long, glides over the grass ocean, like a catamaran in full wind! 400 cadets and post-sea officers are accommodated within five "ships" anchored at either end by the Auditorium (south) and the Catering Centre (north). Aluminium louvres keep the bright sun off of the fenestration and the three Dining Halls are glass prisms facing north, with protective cladded concrete walls to the south and west. The interiors are cast-in-place concrete murals. This long ship floats above the Infinite Corridor, which acts as a covered walkway. The Academic Building is a composition of fourteen large classrooms, with cladded walls to the south and louvred glass. The large lineal atrium connects them all into one composition, with pointed, ship-like porches at either end.

Awarded:
2009, J.K. Cement-Architect of the Year Awards, Best Educational Institute Award
2008, Indian Institute Architects Award, Excellence in Architecture for Best Public Building
2009, Institute of Steel Development & Growth (INSDAG), Runner's up for Best Steel Structure in India
2009, ArchiDesign Awards, Architect of the Year Award
2009, World Architecture Festival Award, Barcelona, Category: Education – Finalist

Top right: Informal cadet's mess adorned with aquatic scenes in exposed RCC
Bottom right: South-facing solar wall generates 90 KW of photovoltaic energy

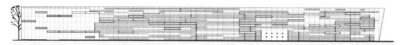

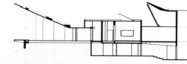

1. Conference
2. Visiting faculty
3. Reception&waiting

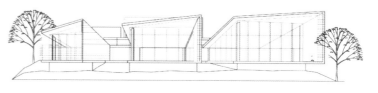

1. Hall
2. Servery
3. Kitchen
4. Kitchen foyer
5. Towards hostel

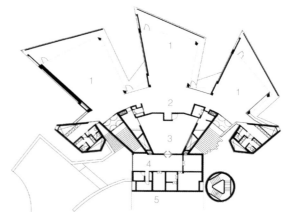

Top left: Main entrance to Academic Centre with louvred facades to cut glare
Top right: Glass wave in atrium shares green landscape
Bottom right: Administration block, with southern photovoltaic wall generating electricity
and mondrian-like façade

Top left: Auditorium wall becomes stage backdrop for amphitheatre
Bottom left: Silo-like stairs hold Floating Hostels to the landscape
Top right: Academic block, interlocking classrooms and landscape
Bottom right: Catering centre opens out to the landscape

LITE Technology Centre

Designer: Eskew+Dumez+Ripple / Guidry Beazley Architects, A Joint Venture **Location:** Louisiana, USA **Completion date:** 2006 **Photographer:** Timothy Hursley

A cooperative endeavour between the Lafayette Economic Development Authority (LEDA) and the University of Louisiana at Lafayette, the Louisiana Immersive Technology Enterprise was conceived as an economic generator for the greater Lafayette region and conceptually developed in 2003-2004. The completed 62,000-square-foot technology centre provides unprecedented research and development opportunities for the State of Louisiana utilising computer visualisation technologies for a wide range of potential clients, from oil and gas exploration companies to university researchers.

In addition to the 40,000 square feet of office space designed for several data technology companies and start-ups, the project contains a variety of high-performance immersion environments including a 200-seat auditorium, two teaching conference rooms and a 3-D visualisation cube called the Total Immersion Space (TIS). It is the first total immersion environment of its kind in the state, and one of only a handful in the nation. The TIS is an advanced 10-x 10-foot, six-sided cube (screens are on each of four walls, ceiling and floor) using multiple projectors in a motion-tracking environment. In order to call attention to the high-performance technology contained within, the client requested that the cube be featured as a prominent visual element within the design. To accomplish this goal, the designers wrapped the self-contained cube within an outer skin of translucent glass. The interstitial space between the glass envelope and the interior cube is illuminated at night, providing an ethereal glow of ever changing coloured light.

Since LITE has such a complicated purpose, the building was designed to simplify its functions. The design strategy was a direct result of translating the different functions into simple forms and wrapping them in different materials and textures. The exterior of the auditorium mass is a solid, cantilevered brick, while the two-storey volume is constructed of brick incorporated with glass. All circulation areas are clad in glass, and equipment and technology areas are wrapped in black zinc.

The cantilever over the entry plaza is clad in Ipe, with several concrete benches lined across from a gradually-sloped water feature clad in the same black zinc.

Right: By day, the glass façades reflect the sky and surrounding natural amenities
Bottom right: The dual-winged building creates an entry plaza that acts as a great overflow space during special events

Awarded:
2008 AIA New Orleans Award of Merit
2008 AIA Gulf States Award of Merit
2007 AIA Louisiana Honour Award
2007 South Central Construction Judge's Award for Design
2007 Louisiana Contractor Judge's Award

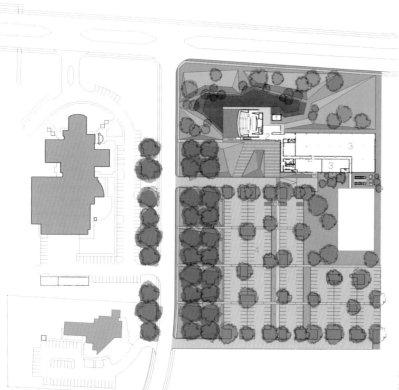

1. Immersive technology space
2. Public space
3. Leasable tenant areas
4. Parking area

Left: From the adjacent roadway, the 3-D cube and reflective cantilever over the retention pond draw visual interest

Top right: The interior lobby, adjacent to the auditorium, is lit almost entirely by natural light by day

Bottom right: The 200-seat auditorium, with desktop surfaces for all attendees, is available for tenant use and often plays host to greater community meetings

Stecca

Designer: 5+1 AA – Alfonso Femia, Gianluca Peluffo **Location:** Milan, Italy **Completion date:** 2006
Photographer: Emesta Caviola, Pietro Savorelli

Frigoriferi Milanesi overlooks this road through a low, long, uninteresting building, which anyway plays a main role from the perspective point of view with respect to the other two important buildings beyond the line. Thanks to its 100 metres length, the building plays with perspective and it points out as a big, bright arrow the entrance to the area, becoming a "Plug Building", an element of communication, connecting the activities taking place inside the area with the city.

The Open Care Café, located in the basement of the "Stecca" overlooking via Piranesi, identifies two territories where it is possible to enjoy the space in different ways: one slow and homelike, with a fireplace; the other fast and urban with a counter made of wood, steel and glass. Two strips of white and glossy resin define the rules for crossing the space, separating the Open Care Café from the road and the outside landscape. The sky is enriched by Bubble-Norlight and the sittings by Sottssas for Segis (Trono). Open Care Café is the new "epi-centrum" of Milan. It is the first entrance to a different world, anticipating the great transformation of Palazzo dei Frigoriferi and Palazzo del Ghiaccio.

Awarded:

2007 "The Colour: Architectonical Material" International Prize

Via Piranesi is characterised by one long and compact front mainly "productive" and another equally fragmented, but "residential".

The lack of personality of the long and low building will be highlighted by two simple processes: on the one hand, a coat of black paint will replace the grey colour, a blob which assails everything: walls, windows, profiles, in order to obliterate any form of architectonic ratiocination and to transform the structure into a black hole, swallowing everything; on the other, a new shiny "skin-peel", made of glass, will be overlapped in order to create a chromatic effect with respect to the monotone geometry of the surrounding area; it unedges the volume with a bi-dimensional and "night" effect.

Left: The new shiny "skin-peel", made of glass, will be overlapped in order to create a chromatic effect with respect to the monotone geometry of the surrounding area

Top right: The Open Care Café is possible to enjoy the space in different ways

Goldener Engel

Designer: Franken Architekturbuero **Location:** Ingelheim, Germany **Completion date:** 2007
Photographer: Franken architekturbuero

The Goldener Engel is a brewery house, positioned among religious buildings, and thus re-interpret the brewery-house tradition. Excitingly the sublime tone of religious buildings and the profane tradition of brewing culture are put in sharp contrast, not to mention between tradition and modernity.

The brewery house, located in Kloster Eberbach on the side of the Rhine, could be dated back to Baroque days, with sharp-edged cross vaulting resting on two sturdy central pillars, reminiscent more of a church nave than a factory hall.

The spatial configuration of the brewery house is a V that runs in one continuous façade strip round a courtyard. The two legs of the V embrace the courtyard, which is thus protected and faces west to the evening sun. The deep wall jambs on the inside trigger interplay of light and shadow, and by running from floor to ceiling, trigger associations with religious places. The courtyard becomes a cloister, with an arcade around it.

The Goldener Engel is so coherent not by superficially quoting traditional brewery houses or trivially borrowing from beer-related clichés, but by using the long-standing tradition of an affinity between places of transformation of matter into finest matter, of meals and evening meals.

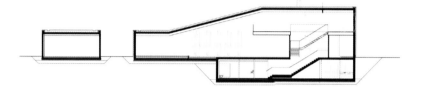

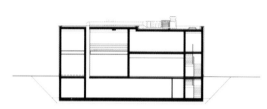

Awarded:
P3D Award "Die goldene Flamme 2007"
2007 DDC Gold Award
2008 ADC Award
2009 Designpreis der BRD Nomination
2008 Leaders Club Award Nomination

In the brewery house, the wall design varies from completely sealed via perforated façades to columned arcades. The open flanks of the folded strip are closed by means of a façade strip. Slits in this façade are positioned according to a rule-based procedure and, reminiscent of local building traditions, enclosed by massive jambs. The façade can be read as a musical score, in which the scale is stated by the height of the slit, the length of the tone by its width, and the rhythm by the distances between the slits. Here, the building references classical temples in Athens, whose columns were set in order determined by the principles of harmony, not to mention Alberti's Renaissance façades, which were devised according to numerical ratios.

Right: Façade strip with musical pattern of openings

Left: Here, the building references classical temples in Athens which were devised according to numerical ratios

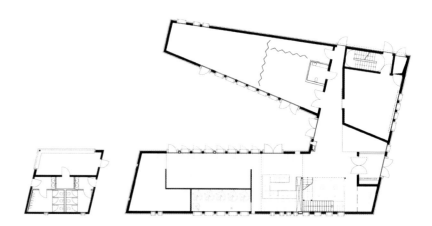

Left: Rough stone texture enhances the tactile experience

Vitali Park

Designer: Cristiano Picco, Jean Pierre Buf **Location:** Turin, Italy **Completion date:** 2008 **Photographer:** Antonella Guerrini

"Vitali Park" is located in via Orvieto, right in the core of "Spina 3", the largest field of contemporary transformation in Turin, where are happening the conversion of important areas occupied by old industries, the creation of a large urban park along the river Dora and the settlement of other important urban functions. The building is designed to hold traditional and innovative productive economic activities, and it is characterised by wide adaptability and flexibility of spaces.

The project's objective is to achieve a high level of environmental comfort in workplaces, from thermal, acoustic and natural lighting viewpoints.

It encompasses two main structures in parallel levels as well as a tall central gallery with transparent roofing. The horizontal connecting system throughout all floors is designed with metal flying bridges hanging to the roofing and balconies looking onto the gallery. The vertical one is structured with staircases blocks inside the buildings' corridors. In addition, a range of loading lifes has been positioned right inside the central covered gallery, functional space and a space relations, completely covered with transparent polycarbonate elements.

This highly structured interior space is in contrast with the homogeneous profile of the eastern and western fronts, being characterised by horizontal terracotta strips with variable scan, mounted on metal profile frames.

The outside longitudinal façades are covered with a "brise-soleil" system in terracotta strips, specifically designed for this project. These strips are mounted on metal profile frames with variable scan (more sparse for transparent parts and more dense for the matt ones).

The northern and southern sides have been made with a complex scan of matt elements (concrete panels) and transparent ones (aluminium window frames), all framed by spandrels in pre-painted metal sheet.

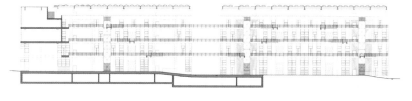

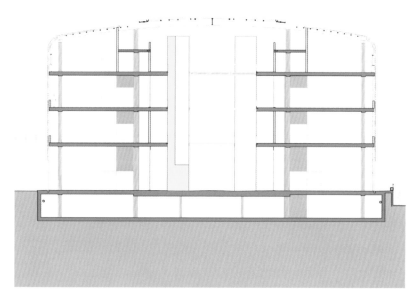

Right: The outside longitudinal façades are covered with a "*brise-soleil*" system in terracotta strips

Awarded:
International Competition

Right: The vertical space is structured with staircases blocks inside the buildings' corridors

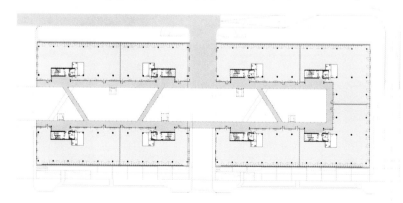

Left: The loading lifts are covered with transparent polycarbonate elements
Right: Transparent roofing

Paykar Bonyan Panel Factory

Designer: ARAD Architechrural Research & Design, Bahram Kalantari, Kourosh Dabbagh **Location:** Tehran, Iran **Completion date:** 2007 **Photographer:** Ali Daghigh, Kamran Adl

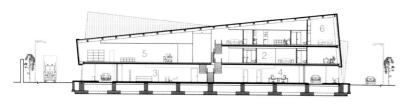

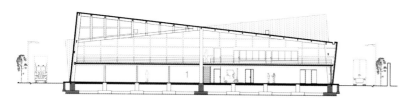

1. Production plant
2. Server room
3. Showroom
4. Accountant office
5. Conference room
6. VIP suit

The project is a factory that contains a prefabricated building system, production plant plus an office & ancillary building. The site location is an industrial city for non-pollution factories, 35 kilometres away from Tehran, Iran. The Client Goal is to change the traditional construction system to an industrial building system which can fulfill the enormous demand of construction in Iran. The client, therefore, wanted the factory to be indicative of this goal in terms of architectural quality in industrial building system with no resemblance to traditional factories in Iran. The programme is a 3,700-square-metre production plant with a 350-square-metre mezzanine for settlement of technical management team and 500-square-metres for technical office and showrooms and mechanical room that must be close to and with a good access to the production plant. There is also a 500-square-metre management building with a VIP suit and receptions that is connected to the main block with a bridge. The ancillary building with 200 square-metres is in a separate building in the site. These types of buildings always possess some characteristics such as large span, modular structure and homogeneous space. Architect's approach towards designing a distinctive building is to bear in mind the above-mentioned characteristics. As regards this project, not only have the characteristic aspects been regarded but also the designers have been able to get the maximum use of a kind of architecture which provides for all quantitative and qualitative architectural demands.

The emphasis was to apply a simple geometry of space to be able to meet all the prospects foreseen in the project such as the programme and the required connectivity, and moreover be able to create a new atmosphere which makes turn a globe either in section or in plan as well as the project façade (interior and exterior) into a homogeneous object. The building is located North-South lengthwise and the main administration building which overlooks Alborz mountain has a uniform glass view.

Top right: North façade at night
Bottom right: East façade – office passage way

Awarded:
"Memar awards first prize" Memar magazine, no. 46, December – January 2007-2008
World Architecture Festival 2008 – Shortlisted

Left: Technical platform – interior
Top right: Production plant interior with the entry of indirect light
Bottom right: Central staircase in the offices

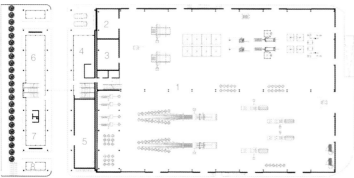

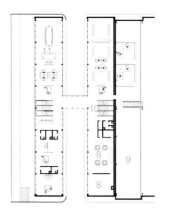

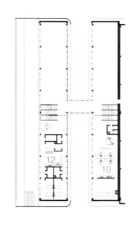

1. Production plant
2. Electrical room
3. Storage
4. Server room
5. Mechanical room
6. Showroom
7. Accountant office
8. Guard
9. Production mezzanine
10. Technical office
11. Conference room
12. VIP suite

CUSWC – Central Urban Solid Waste Collection

Designer: Vaíllo & Irigaray + Galar **Location:** Navarra, Spain **Completion date:** 2009 **Photographer:** Jose M. Cutillas

A CUSWC — Central Urban Solid Waste Collection - is a big urban stomach. It aspires all kinds of waste from where they originate, the swallows, separate and compact trucks to evacuate through the various points of treatment, reuse and recycling. Vacuuming and compacting are the specific tasks of the plant.

A big sucker managed to introduce waste into the plant through a pipeline, which works greatly as a small city.

The compact package waste classified in different formats minimised geometric volume.

It also functions as and a great waste finisher, allowing different types of treatment and recycling.

A CUSWC is a clean building, a building able to coexist with other uses of a city is not a building that has to hide, but most of them are factory buildings, industrial, "blind", insensitive to environment. In this sense the designers wanted the central bio-morphic traits, to be able to accentuate its personality for coexistence: it is a building that looks and smells; it has a nose and eyes.

Its own inner workings, however, require a noisy guts building: it is necessary to generate a building with different shells and layers of noise protection. A recognisable coating fitted with a scale capable of being liken by some form of mimesis, perhaps conceptually adds to the peculiarities of place and "culture" to be generated: ecological culture, a "green culture".

The contorted volumetric flakes wrapped with the same material, same construction system, and façades and deck-large format sheets (2.5mx1.5m) are composed of leaf-lacquered aluminium that can recycle, with minimum thickness. The construction system of the coating is based on a process of "optimisation of the coating material" and therefore makes its own strain on the thin veneer: it allows and encourages such a strain to generate an image of "scales swollen" capable to provide the appropriate scale to the composition of the pieces that make up the volume, while recalling that all digestion generates swelling due to internal gas of the process. The image of "patchwork" of focusing the intensity is desired in the iconography.

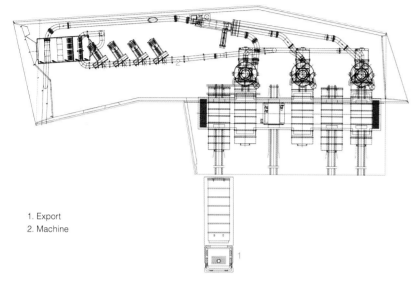

1. Export
2. Machine

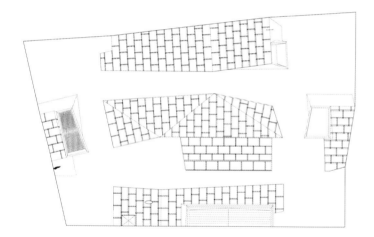

Right: The building is able to coexist with other uses of the city

Awarded:
COAVN Awards Finalist 2010

Right: A recognisable coating fitted with a scale capable of being likened by some form of mimesis

Roseisle Distillery

Designer: Austin-Smith:Lord **Location:** Morayshire, UK **Completion date:** 2009 **Photographer:** Keith Hunter Photography

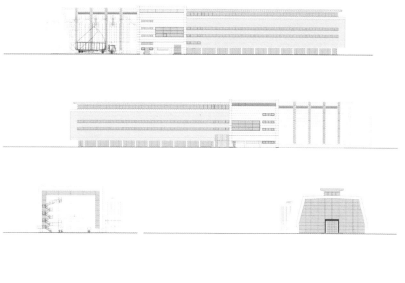

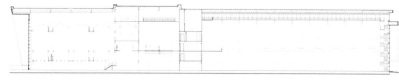

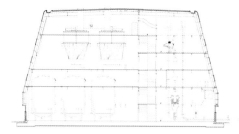

Diageo's new £40m malt whisky distillery in Roseisle, Morayshire, is the first major distillery built in Scotland for 30 years. Designed by award-winning, international design practice, Austin-Smith:Lord, the rural distillery, with a potential output of 10 million litres of malt whisky per year, combines centuries of accumulated distilling knowledge and expertise with cutting-edge design and technology. Whilst accommodating traditional distilling techniques, the distillery was designed to be highly energy-efficient and technically advanced, as well as architecturally sensitive to its visual and environmental impact.

The building is a modern interpretation of the traditional still house and maximises natural ventilation and daylight. The architects worked closely with Diageo's production team and consulting engineers, AECOM, to accommodate evolving designs. Stack-effect natural ventilation was incorporated into the design to reduce overheating within the still house (air is introduced at low-level and expelled at high-level) and some hot water is recovered for use in the maltings. A water reclamation plant aims to recycle 300,000m³ of liquid produced by the distillery as potable water, thus helping to replenish its intake. The draff (grain remaining after mashing) is used as biomass fuel to generate the steam that charges the stills, reducing potential CO_2 emissions by approximately 13,000 tonnes through direct savings on fuel use for steam raising.

The impressive plant sizes dictated the overall scale of the building's 3,000m² gross internal area. The layout and massing of the building express the three main processes of whisky-making-mashing, fermentation and distilling. Each section was afforded a distinct volume and architectural style. For architectural reasons, the mash house was designed with a higher roof than necessary in order to maintain the proportionality of the building, and a "cathedral space" was created within the still house, and the 8-metre-high copper stills are displayed like highly crafted sculptural objects.

Awarded:
(Royal Institute of Chartered Surveyors) RICS Scotland 2010 Awards – Sustainability Project of the Year / Overall Project of the Year
Scottish Design Award 2010 – Commercial Project Category

Top right: ThermoWood cladding on the Still House (south elevation)
Bottom right: View of the distillery from southwest

Left: Internal Tank Farm (looking west)
Top right: Still House on the third floor (looking east)
Bottom right: Detail of the tuba-like copper stills (looking east) and the Still House with a window to the Conference Room at the end wall

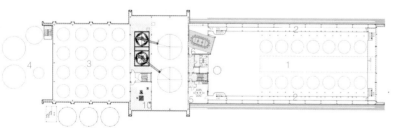

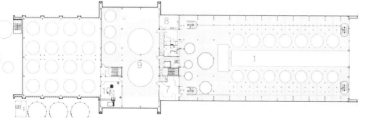

1. Still House
2. Access Gantry
3. Tank Farm 1
4. Tank Farm 2
5. Meeting Room
6. Board Room
7. Control Room
8. Mess Room
9. Mash House
10. Mill Room

Rossignol World Headquarters

Designer: Hérault Arnod **Location:** Villages of la Buisse and Saint-Jean-de-Moirans, France
Completion date: 2009 **Photographer:** André Morin, Gilles Cabella

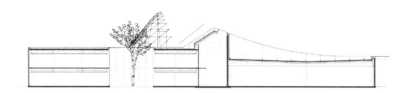

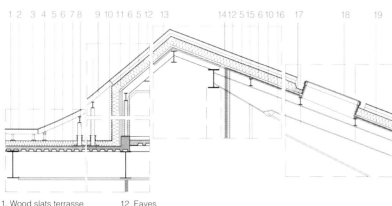

1. Wood slats terrasse
2. Wood Joist
3. Plot PVC
4. Joist fixed with studs
5. Sealing
6. Insulation and vapor barrier
7. Composite floor
8. Candle support of overroof
9. Chevron wood
10. Angle bead
11. Support metal or wood
12. Eaves
13. Overroof wood blade 60x22mm
14. Overroof wood blade 140x22mm
15. Girder
16. Metal beam subtended
17. Folded sheet
18. Canopy
19. Perforated wood ceiling

The image of Rossignol, a historic leader in the world of skiing, is intimately linked with the mountains and with snow. The project for its worldwide headquarters has nothing to do with the stereotypical office building, but is in harmony with nature and the peaks, and at the same time with technology, which is inseparable from high-level sport. The plot stands in the middle of a plain surrounded by mountains. It is a stretch of former farmland, marshy and perfectly flat, bounded on the northern side by the Lyon/Grenoble motorway. The architecture has been designed specifically for Rossignol, a fusion of the company's functional and imaginative aspects, in a radical and minimalist form: it is inspired by board sports, by fluidity of motion, and also by reliefs, snow and glacier sculpted by the elements. The roof, which envelops the whole project, is a topography in osmosis with the landscape. Its organic, timber-clad shape echoes the profile of the mountains that surround the site.

The company needed to create the "home of Rossignol", a place to unite the different entities that had spread across the country as the company grew.

On the motorway side, the façade creates a kinetic and dynamic effect, curving upwards to form a roof over the workshops and then on to the apex, before descending again on the southwestern side to cover the office area. It is then broken up with shale-paved patios planted with magnolias, so that nature and building overlap in an interplay of the transparencies. The irregular profile of the roof and office façades leave the opportunity for future extensions as required. Additions can be built without disrupting the balance and identity of the project. From the start, the architecture embodies its own growth process. The roof ridge, with a glasshouse running along it, is positioned above the street, an elevated space giving onto the "high-altitude restaurant", the highest point of the structure, a reminder of ski slope restaurants.

Inside, the building functions like a "hive" in which the different activities intersect and communicate. The originality of the programme is that it unites very different functions, from production to services, under a single roof. The aim of this assembly is to create a global synergy which prevents barriers between design, service and technology. Each person in their diversity – engineer, designer, technician, secretary, salesman, etc. – meets in reciprocal encounter. To encourage this internal communication, social spaces are distributed around the building. The restaurant, situated right at the top and at the centre of gravity of the street, is designed as the primary nucleus of company life: two great glasshouses divide up the panoramic views to the sky and the mountains, on one side to the Vercors and on the other to the Chartreuse. A large roof terrace is provided for alfresco lunching, protected from the noise of the motorway.

Only two materials are used for the external envelope: wood (natural larch) and glass. The structure is made of steel, like an organic skeleton that outlines the shape with its many warped surfaces. The roof frame is visible in the workshop and offices. The post-and-beam frame of the service floors spans distances of 12 to 16 metres to leave the space as free as possible.

Awarded:
Grand Prix SIMI

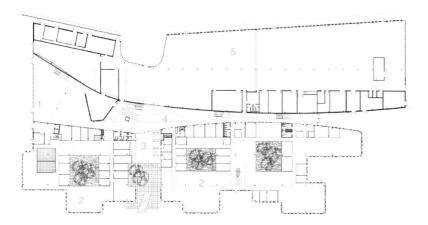

1. Showroom
2. Bureaux
3. Hall
4. Road
5. Atelier

Top left: Restaurant
Bottom right: Open-space offices

Left: Lift
Top right: Showroom
Bottom right: Factory

Index

Equator Stockholm AB
phone: +46 08 50 60 25 00
fax: +46 08 50 60 25 99

Arkhefield
Phone: +61 07 3831 8150

Atkins
Phone: +44 01905 338247

KPF
phone: +1 212 977 6500
fax: +1 212 956 2526

Foreign Office Architects
phone: +44 207 033 9800
fax: +44 207 033 9801

Cepezed Architects
phone: +31 15 2150000
fax: +31 15 2130908

Henning Larsen Architects
phone: +45 8233 3000
fax: +45 8233 3099

Parque Humano
phone: +52 55 5281 7640
fax: +52 55 5281 7641

Elkus Manfredi Architects
phone: +1 617 426 1300

3DReid
phone: +44 (0)289 043 6970
fax: +44 (0)289 043 6699

Tony Owen
phone: +61 2 96982900
fax: +61 2 96993018

Ross Barney Architects
phone: +1 312 832 0600
fax: +1 312 832 0601

Gerd Bergmeister Architekten
phone: +39 0472 801129
fax: +39 334 6082704

Jensen Architects
phone: +1 415 348 9650
fax: +1 415 348 9651

Stan Allen Architects
phone: +1 718 624 7827

Progetto CMR
phone: +39 02 584909 1
fax: +39 02 584909 20

Integrated Architecture
phone: +1 616 574 0220
fax: +1 616 574 0953

Mei Architecten
phone: +31 (0)10 4252222

DeStefano Partners
phone: +1 312 836 4321
fax: +1 312 836 4322

Fentress Architects
phone: +303 722 500021

Riegler Riewe Architekten
phone: +43 316 72 32 53
fax: +43 316 72 32 53 4

Art&Build Architects
phone: +32 2 538 72 71
fax: +32 2 538 65 57

BURO II
phone:+61 3 9670 1966
fax: +61 3 9670 1955

Charles Barclays Architects
phone: +44 020 8674 0037
fax: +44 020 8683 9696

Promontorio Architects
phone: +35 1 218 620 970
fax: +35 1 218 620 971

J.Mayer.H
phone: +49 (0)30 644 90 77 00
fax: +49 (0)30 644 90 77 11

Stanley Saitowitz I Natoma Architects
phone: +41 5 701 7900
fax: +41 5 626 8978

Hudson Architects
phone: +44 1 603 766 220
fax: +44 1 603 766 220

JKMM Architects
phone: +35 8 9 2522 0700
fax: +35 8 9 2522 0710

G.Natkeviius, E.Spd
phone: +370 37 320814
fax: +370 37 320814

STUDIO UP
phone: +385 1 3789996
fax: +385 1 3789998

AK2
phone: +421 2 544 16 162
fax: +421 907 65 55 05

OFIS arhitekti
phone: +386 1 4260084
fax: +386 1 4260085

Gmp Architekten
phone: +49 (0)40 88 151 -0
fax: +49 (0)40 88 151 -177

MGP Arquitecturay Urbanismo
phone: +57 1 6912858

Elkus Manfredi Architects
phone: +1 617 426 1300

Saucier + Perrotte Architectes
phone: +1 514 273 1700
fax: +1 514 273 3501

KlingStubbins
phone: +86 10 59004157
fax: +86 10 59004159

Hawkins \ Brown
phone: +44 020 7336 8030
fax: +44 020 7336 8851

Christopher Charles Benninger Architects Pvt. Ltd
phone: +91 20 65102331

Eskew+Dumez+Ripple
phone: +1 504 561 8686
fax: +1 504 522 2253

5+1 AA
phone: +39 010 540095
fax: +39 010 5702094

Franken Architekturbuero
phone: +49 69 297 2830

Picco architetti
phone: +39 011 539416

ARAD Architechrural Research & Design
phone: +98 21 2201 0203
fax: +98 21 2204 5561

Vaíllo & Irigaray + Galar
phone: +34 94 8290054
fax: +34 94 8290303

Austin-Smith:Lord
phone: +44 (0)2920 225 208

Hérault Arnod
phone: +33 (0) 4 76 12 94 94
fax: +33 (0) 4 76 86 11 44

©2010 by Design Media Publishing Limited
This edition published in July 2011

Design Media Publishing Limited
20/F Manulife Tower
169 Electric Rd, North Point
Hong Kong
Tel: 00852-28672587
Fax: 00852-25050411
E-mail: Kevinchoy@designmediahk.com
www.designmediahk.com

Editing: Arthur Gao
Proofreading: Maggie Wang
Design/Layout: Cong Zhao

ISBN 978-988-19740-0-6

Printed in China